German Armoured Cars
of World War Two

German Armoured Cars of World War Two

John Milsom &
Peter Chamberlain

PSB Book Club Edition

Published in 1974 by
Arms and Armour Press
Lionel Leventhal Limited
2–6 Hampstead High Street
London NW3 1PR

© Lionel Leventhal Limited, 1974
© John Milson and Peter
    Chamberlain. 1974
Reprinted 1976
ISBN 85368 239 9

This edition published by
Purnell Book Services Ltd, St. Giles
House, 49/50 Poland Street,
London W1A 2LG, by arrangement
with Arms & Armour Press.

Printed by T. & A. Constable Limited, Edinburgh

Contents

Introduction

1. Early Developmental Types

During the late 1920s, the Germans began secret experiments with new models of armoured fighting vehicles. The terms of the Versailles Treaty forbade them tactical vehicles of any description, which was why new vehicles had to be kept highly secret. With the signing of the Rapallo Agreement between the Soviet Union and Germany, however, an experimental armoured-vehicle testing station was established at Kazan, on the Volga, where German and Soviet personnel collaborated in the development of technology and tactics. German participation at Kazan was directly controlled by General Hans von Seeckt, Chef der Heeresleitung, and the actual testing section was under the command of Hauptmann Pirner. This new facility opened up great possibilities for the development of German armoured vehicles. But because all German developmental vehicles had to be constructed in German factories, they had to be of ambiguous design if they were not to attract the attention of Allied observers.

Consequently, tracked armoured fighting vehicles were referred to as 'Traktoren' (tractors) and armoured cars were called 'Gepanzerter Mannschaftstransportwagenen' (armoured personnel carriers). Contrary to popular belief, the German prototype armoured cars tested at Kazan were wheeled tanks—not armoured reconnaissance cars. The designation 'Panzerspähwagen' (armoured reconnaissance vehicle) did not evolve until the formulation of the Panzer Division concept several years later. Indeed, the Germans have never adopted a designation that clearly distinguishes between wheeled and tracked armoured vehicles.

During 1926-7, the Reichswehrministerium/Heereswaffenamt Wa. Prüf.6 (Prüfwesen 6) prepared the basic specifications for the new Mannschaftstransportwagen after various road and cross-country trials with commercial vehicles. These specifications were as follows:

1. The vehicle must have wheels (six or more, with multiple wheel drive).

2. On good, level roads a maximum speed of 65kph (40mph) should be achieved, the minimum allowable speed being 5kph (3mph). A day's motoring of 200kms (125miles) at an average speed of 32kph (20mph) must be sustained for three successive days.

3. The vehicle must be capable of negotiating the worst terrain. The ground pressure, at a slope angle of up to 80°, must not exceed 0.7kg/sq.cm (10psi).

4. On arable land, the vehicle must be able to negotiate grades of up to 1 in 3.

5. The vehicle must be able to cross trenches up to 1.5m (4.92ft) wide without the aid of special devices and without stalling.

6. The vehicle must be able to wade to a depth of up to 1m (3.3ft).

7. The vehicle should possess the same driving characteristics for forward and reverse. For each driving direction, special steering facilities are required. The changeover from one direction to the other must be achieved by the driver within ten seconds.

8. The turning circle radius must not exceed four times the track.

9. With sustained motoring, the vehicle should make very little sound.

10. The chassis weight must not exceed 4 tons, and the overall weight of the ready-to-drive vehicle must not be greater than 7.5 tons.

11. The ground clearance must be at least 0.3m (1ft).

12. The vehicle must be capable of driving along standard-guage railway tracks. Special provisions to cater for this must not be used, but the track width should be such that the inner wheel rims will fit the rails.

13. [This section, concerning amphibious characteristics, was subsequently amended. It stipulated that the vehicle should be capable of floating without special preparation and be able to move through the water at a speed of 5kph (3mph).]

14. The crew is to consist of five men, as follows: commander; driver; first gunner; second gunner; radio-operator (also acting as rear driver).

All of the other points enumerated in this specification were in connection with technical components such as the engine, gearbox, steering system, brakes, suspension and wheels. Careful attention was also paid to the effective application of armour and armament— the Germans being very impressed not only by Czech armour application but also by the weapon mountings and optics utilised in Swedish armoured fighting vehicles.

The specifically individual requirements demanded of new armoured-car models made the use of commercially available chassis impossible. It was therefore necessary for tenders to be issued to leading German automobile manufacturers for vehicles corresponding to these demands—the selection of the participating firms being made with great caution. Only those based solely in Germany were approached. This was to avoid the sort of security leaks that could occur between home-based companies and their overseas subsidiaries —as might have been the case with, for example, Ford.

Eventually, development contracts were given to three firms—Daimler-Benz A.G., Stuttgart-Untertürkheim; C. D. Magirus, Ulm/Donau; and Büssing-NAG, Braunschweig (Brunswick)—all of whom, during 1929, delivered prototypes that were variously tested at Kazan, Kummersdorf and Wünsdorf. Magirus and Daimler-Benz were involved in 8-wheeled designs, and Büssing-NAG concerned itself with a 10-wheeled model.

The Daimler-Benz 8-wheeled ARW/MTW 1 Gespanzerter Mannschaftstransportwagen

The Daimler-Benz model was known as the ARW/MTM 1 (Achtradwagen/Mannschaftstransportwagen, or Eight-Wheeled Vehicle/Personnel Carrier)—a designation calculated to disguise the fact that it was really an armoured car or wheeled tank. Design work was carried out at the factory at Stuttgart-Untertürkheim under the direction of Professor Ferdinand Porsche. Two prototype vehicles were completed, both possessing remarkable features and giving excellent performance for that time.

The automotive components were produced at the Stuttgart plant, and the die-formed and welded hulls were constructed by Martini und Hünecke in Salzkotten. The turret installation, the turret traversing gear and the armament mountings were produced by Rheinmetall in Düsseldorf, but they were never fitted to the vehicles. Assembly was carried out by Daimler-Benz at their Berlin-Marienfelde plant.

The vehicles had eight-wheel drive and fully independent suspension on all wheels, which were suspended direct from the armoured body and thus eliminated the need for a chassis frame. Steering was on the front and rear pair of wheels only, the centre ones being slewed round. For this reason, the centre wheels were grouped in a similar fashion to those of the Austrian ADGZ armoured car.

One of the prototypes was fitted with a parallelepidal cork body, primarily to hide the true nature of the vehicle but also to assist buoyancy, but in all other respects the two were identical. The body was almost symmetrical and of smooth, rounded-off design to reduce

drag in water and to enhance ballistic qualities; and had the turret been fitted it would have been almost hemispherical in shape.

To cater for both forward and reverse driving, duplicated steering positions and controls were provided. The design of the rear steering system was such that the steering column and all hand and foot brakes were removable from the rear driver's seat. This was considered necessary in order to deceive the Inter-Allied Control Commission. Water propulsion was by means of a propeller, which could be engaged by a hand lever.

At the end of 1930, after extensive test drives, the vehicle was delivered to the Reichswehr.

Characteristics
Overall laden weight: 7800/6200kg[1].
Crew: Five men (as in original specification).
Length, overall: 5450mm.
Width, overall: 2280mm.
Height, overall: 2135/1350mm[1].
Ground clearance: 300mm.
Track, front and rear wheels: 1800mm[2].
Wheelbase: 1550+1160+1550mm (total 4260mm).
Engine
Make: Daimler-Benz (petrol).
Model: M-36 (in two units).
No. of cylinders: 6 (in-line).
Output: 105hp at 2350rpm.
Swept volume: 7793cc.
Cooling: Water.
Transmission, land
Five forward and five reverse gears[3]; gear-shifting was carried out by one lever each from both drivers' seats. When reversing, another lever (one near each driver's seat) had to be engaged. The eight wheels were driven by a worm gear from the central drive-shaft. The differential gear was situated in every axle between right and left.
Transmission, water
Special selector gear for bringing into operation a two-bladed propeller (800mm diameter). Two ratios— one forward and one reverse.
Clutch: Multi-disc, dry plate.
Steering: Two screw-and-nut systems, the four outer wheels being steered. The front and rear wheels were coupled to each other by one crown wheel and bevel pinion and one rotary selector each.
Brakes: Hydraulic four-wheel internal shoe-brake that acted on the inner four wheels; two separate hydraulic brake systems, actuated by one brake pedal each from both drivers' seats. The hand-brake acted on a brake on the transmission shaft attached to the change unit.
Chassis: The vehicle had no frame; the armoured body carried the drive-chain and wheels.
Suspension: Semi-elliptic longitudinal leaf-springs; all wheels were independently suspended (floating axles with guide shoes). Wheels were sheet discs and tyres were 40cm x 8cm[4].
Armour: Die-formed and welded armour steel, proof against small-calibre bullets beyond 25 metres. Front, 13.5mm-15mm; roof, 5mm; other surfaces, 13.5mm.

Armament: One 37mm Rheinmetall semi-automatic gun, and one 7.92mm machine-gun, coaxially mounted in a turret with all-round traverse.
Ammunition: 66 rounds 37mm, 1000 rounds 7.62 mm.
Performance
Maximum speed, land: 65kph (forward and reverse).
Maximum speed, water: 5kph (forward and reverse).
Cruising speed (land): 32kph.
Fuel capacity: 170 litres.
Range, road: 200-250km.
Range, cross-country: 150km.
Range, water: 6 hours duration.
Turning circle diameter: 14.4m.
Trench crossing ability: 1.5m.
Grade ability: 18°.
Wading depth (before flotation): 1000mm.

Notes: 1. With/without turret. 2. 1812mm fully laden. 3. Later Aphon, four forward and four reverse. 4. Originally 1060 x 200.

The Büssing-NAG 10-wheeled ZRW Mannschaftstransportwagen

The Büssing-NAG vehicle had ten independently suspended wheels, all of which were driven. They were grouped in two units of four—one unit at each end—with the remaining two wheels mounted on a centrally-located axle. The amoured hull—like that of the Daimler-Benz model, to which it was very similar—was produced by Martini und Hünecke in Salzkotten. A light steel girdle was riveted around the hull to disguise its prominent military shape. Each of the four-wheel units was steered; but in the one prototype built, only one steering position was incorporated at the centre of the hull. The steering wheel was attached to a vertical column with two locating points so that the wheel could be attached for driving in either direction. Due to its location, however, the steering position did not provide a very good view of the road. On trials, the driver often had to stand upright in order to see. The water-cooled Büssing engine was mounted at one end of the vehicle, and the transmission system and drive shafts for the water propulsion screws were located at the other end. The hull above the experimental superstructure was completed, but nothing is known concerning a proposed turret installation—although it is most likely that the Rheinmetall installation intended for the Daimler-Benz model would eventually have been used. The performance and steering characteristics of the vehicle left much to be desired, however, and during its maiden amphibious trial in Russia it sank.

The Migirus ARW/MTW 2 8-wheeled Gepanzerter Mannschaftstransportwagen

This vehicle was of very similar design to the Daimler-Benz model; but since neither photographs nor technical data have come to light, it is not known whether it was actually completed.

Trials and Conclusions

The Heereswaffenamt appeared to be particularly inter-ested in the Daimler-Benz vehicle and was quite satisfied with the results of its trials. But because of the bad industrial situation that existed during 1929/30, neither the manufacture of special all-wheel-drive vehicles for the conversion of commercial models to suit the technical requirements seemed possible.

A conference held on 18th March 1930 under Reimann of Wa.Prüf.6 concluded that 'the further pursuance of this type of vehicle is considered to be out of the question, since the present financial status of the Reich makes vehicles of this size and type far too expensive.'

---

2. The Evolution of the Panzerspähwagen (armoured reconnaissance car)

During the late twenties and early thirties, experimental exercises were carried out in Germany to study the requirements of a modern mechanised army. Because of the non-availability of armoured fighting vehicles, a series of Panzernachbildung (simulated armoured fighting vehicles) was produced—representing both tanks and armoured cars—on commercial-vehicle chassis. These helped to determine the requirements of the Wehrmacht. Several such dummy armoured cars were built on Hanomag and Dixi chassis. In simulation of the Czech PA-2 (referred to by the Germans as the Schildkröte, or turtle—not to be confused with the Schildkröte amphibious armoured car projects developed by Hans Trippel), a commercial lorry chassis was used. This vehicle took part in exercises near Hannover in 1928.

In 1930 the Reichswehr received a simulated armoured car of aluminium plate—later of thin mild-steel—based on the chassis of the Adler Standard 6 car. This vehicle had a rotating turret with a simulated stroboscope, and the vehicle-commander and gunner stood on a rotating footstool. Next to the driver, in the passenger seat, sat the radio-operator. The vehicle was prominent in the Elsgrund-district exercises of 1930. During 1935 a further dummy armoured car was built on the chassis of the Opel P4—(and as late as 1941 a dummy training car based on the Volkswagen Type 82 chassis was in service).

Many valuable conclusions concerning armoured reconnaissance were drawn from the experimental exercises, and it was stated that one of the first duties of the 'fast troops'—to be carried out before opposing forces had actually joined battle—was reconnaissance. Reconnaissance provided the High Command with the information needed for further operations and air reconnaissance was not always sufficient for the purpose—particularly as it often could not determine whether ground was occupied by the enemy and, if so, in what strength. Here ground reconnaissance began; and it was broken down into operational reconnaissance, tactical reconnaissance and battle reconnaissance.

Operational reconnaissance was the duty of the high units, from corps upwards; tactical reconnaissance was carried out by divisions and smaller units, and battle reconnaissance was the smallest units responsibility.

According to General Guderian, reconnaissance called for especially fast, flexible and easily commanded units with a wide field of action and good communications. They had to see and report a good deal without being observed; and for this reason, the smaller and the more easily concealed they were the better they could perform their task. Their strength had to be so gauged that it could prevail against an enemy of similar formation; and if their duties called for additional fighting power, it would have to be given to them as required. The instrument of modern ground reconnaissance was the scout car and several scout cars made up an armoured reconnaissance detachment. The establishment of armoured reconnaissance detachments would vary in respect of duties and the number and types of vehicles; but they would as a rule, include two or three companies of light and heavy armoured cars.

In addition to air observation, operational reconnaissance was carried out by special ground units—the reconnaissance detachments, whose special function was to discover enemy concentrations and march routes, railway transports and fortified points. They were the modern equivalent of cavalry, with the advantage of a larger radius of action and greater fighting strength since they consisted almost entirely of motorised forces. All of their vehicles were wireless-equipped (initially, only special communications vehicles had long-range radio equipment) and could therefore report directly to the command if occasion demanded. These reconnaissance detachments were at the exclusive disposal of the larger units.

The needs of divisional intelligence were mainly served by detachments with similar technical equipment but whose function was tactical reconnaissance, covering a more restricted area than operational units and only fully motorised in the case of motorised divisions.

Armoured reconnaissance forces were often the first to establish contact with the enemy; but a reconnaissance troop was not, by its nature, suited for offensive operations. At most, it was capable of sustained (not permanent) defence.

Battle reconnaissance was intended to furnish information on the situation of a battle while it was actually being fought. It was neither operational nor tactical.

As far as vehicles were concerned, the following military specifications were laid down as additional to or amending the original ones issued during 1926-7:
1. High road and, wherever possible, cross-country speeds.
2. Reasonable cross-country mobility.
3. Relatively large radii of action.
4. Long-range radio communication.
5. Protection from small-arms fire.
6. Armament suitable for delaying actions only.

During 1938, special armoured reconnaissance units were formed within the framework of the Panzer and Panzergrenadier divisions—the Panzerdivision Aufklarungsabteilung (armoured division reconnaissance unit) and the Infanteriedivision Aufklarungsabteilung (infantry division reconnaissance unit).

The armoured division had a reconnaissance unit containing an armoured car squadron, three armoured reconnaissance companies, and support weapons grouped in a heavy company. This formation was really the spearhead of the division, moving forward along all possible tracks ahead of the division to weed out resistance, brush aside weak opposition, and seize bridgeheads, road junctions, towns and villages. Its task was to obtain information about the enemy and his dispositions, thus enabling the divisional commander to formulate his plan of attack. An armoured reconnaissance unit was composed of a headquarters, a headquarters company, an armoured-car squadron and three armoured reconnaissance companies.

The Mechanised Reconnaissance Unit

The armoured division would send out a mechanised reconnaissance unit in directions where air reconnaissance needed rapid supplementation and where a clear picture of the enemy's positions could be gained only by fighting. The unit, specially equipped for this with armoured cars and a large number of automatic weapons, could move fast and had a wide radius of action. It was capable of being employed up to 100km (60 miles) ahead of the division. The frontage on which a reconnaissance was carried out would generally be laid down by corps and could extend to as much as 60 miles. On open flanks it would frequently be even wider.

As there were so many possible reconnaissance tasks, it was imperative for commanders to concentrate on essentials. Apart from tasks for which any reconnaissance unit could be utilised, the mechanised reconnaissance unit in particular had to give warning of enemy anti-tank defences and prepare the way for the movements and operations of the division.

As soon as battle was joined, the mechanised reconnaissance unit would be told whether it was to continue reconnoitring, temporarily hold commanding features, withdraw to or through the division, move off the front, or reconnoitre to the flanks. It was not made up to a strength that could carry out defensive tasks. An open flank, for example, could be covered by long-range reconnaissance but had to be protected by other troops.

Allocation of Armoured Cars

	Heavy	Light
Armoured Division		
Reconnaissance unit	12	42
Lorried infantry brigade	4	8
Infantry Division		
Reconnaissance unit	—	3
Motorised Division		
Reconnaissance unit	6	18

▲1   2▼

Daimler Benz 8-wheeled ARW/MTW 1

1. Prototype with armoured body and wooden frame surrounding the turret ring.

2. During cross-country trials.

3. Fitted with a cork body. On this vehicle, seen during cross-country trials, the propeller for water-propulsion is clearly discernible.

4. The amphibious version during water trials.

5. Wooden model of the proposed ARW/MTW 1, complete, showing the hemispherical turret. The water-propulsion propeller is also evident.

▲ 3

▲ 4   5 ▼

Büssing-NAG 10-wheeled ZRW
6. Prototype with superstructure surrounding the armoured body.
7. With the upper part of the hull removed to disclose the automotive components and controls.
8. During amphibious trials in Russia.

Panzer Nachbildung
9. A very early version simulating a machine-gun tank.
10. An early version taking part in an exercise.

▲ 6

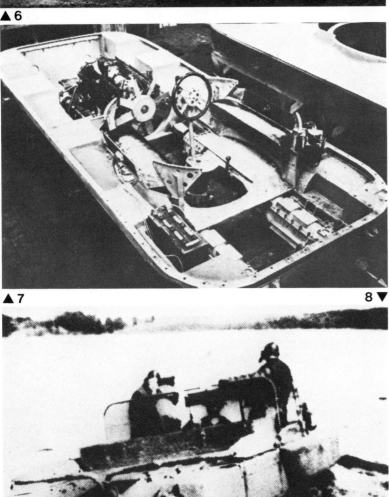

▲ 7   8 ▼

▲ 9

10 ▼

Panzer Nachbildung
11, 12. Early version, simulating artillery tanks, taking part in an exercise in the early thirties.
13. A later version simulating a Panzerkampfwagen I light tank.

Adler Standard 6
14. Simulated armoured car. Note the stroboscope on the rear of the turret.
15. On a reconnaissance exercise.

▲ 11

▲ 12   13 ▼

▲16

17▼

Adler Standard 6

16. Simulated armoured cars of a reconnaissance group during an exercise.

17. Simulated Czech 'Schildkröte' PA-2 armoured car taking part in an exercise.

2. Four-wheeled vehicles

1. Mittlerer Gepanzerter Personenkraftwagen (medium armoured passenger car) 4 x 2 Adler (Kfz.13 series)

This was a medium 4 x 2 armoured car based on the chassis of the widely-used Adler Standard 6 Küblesitzer passenger car—although it is said that some of these vehicles were built around the Adler Standard 3U chassis. It was built to a military requirement issued by the Reichsministerium/Heereswaffenamt during 1932, when the German Army required a light armoured wheeled vehicle of a type not yet in existence. Being inexpensive and easy to produce, it appeared in relatively large numbers after 1934 and was issued to cavalry regiments until the appearance of newer versions in 1937. It is believed that even as early as 1932 the car was never intended to represent the ideal reconnaissance car but was purely an expedient until funds became available for the production of a more efficient and more versatile vehicle.

During 1933 Daimler-Benz, in Berlin-Marienfelde, acted as parent firm for the vehicle; and the armoured body was the responsibility of Deutschen Edelstahl, in Hannover-Linden.

The vehicle had a front-located 3-litre, 6-cylinder, in-line engine developing 60hp at 3200rpm. A sliding-pinion 4-speed gearbox drove the conventional rear axle; and the hull, of welded construction, was box-shaped.

Closely resembling a sports car, the vehicle had curved mudguards. Its rigid wheel suspension was by semi-elliptic leaf springs, and only the front pair of wheels was steered.

With a two-man crew and machine-gun armament the vehicle's official designation was MG-Kw (Kfz.13) Maschinengewehrkraftwagen mit Fahrgestell des mittleren Personenkraftwagen (0)—machine-gun vehicle with the chassis of the medium passenger car, commercial. With a three-man crew and radio equipment it was Fu-Kw (Kfz.14) Funkkraftwagen mit Fahrgestell des mittleren Personenkraftwagen (0)—wireless vehicle with the chassis of the medium passenger car, commercial.

The Kfz.13s carried no radio equipment, communication being by means of flags alone. But this was not considered much of a handicap since they were always accompanied by a Kfz.14 with its long-range wireless-telegraphy and radio-telegraphy transmitter and receiver—the aerial for which was of a frame type and could be folded down around the vehicle when not in use. Because of the bulk of its radio equipment—which had a range of about twenty miles—the Kfz.14 mounted no armament. Both models were open-topped and protected all round by 8mm armour, their construction representing one of the earliest German attempts at welding armour plate.

The Kfz.13 fulfilled the 'Waffenwagen' (weapons-carrier) role and was armed with a 7.92mm MG-13

Characteristics	Kfz.13	Kfz.14
Weight, unladen:	1900kg (1.9 tons)	1900kg (1.9 tons)
Weight, fully laden:	2200kg (2.2 tons)	2250kg (2.3 tons)
Crew:	2 men	3 men
Length, overall:	4200mm (13.78ft)	4200mm (13.78ft)
Width, overall:	1700mm (5.56ft)	1700mm (5.56ft)
Height, overall:	1500mm (4.91ft)	1500mm (4.91ft) *
Ground clearance:	180mm (7.1in)	180mm (7.1in)
Track—front and rear:	1430mm (4.69ft)	1430mm (4.69ft)
Wheelbase:	2840mm (9.31ft)	2840mm (9.31ft)
Wheel width:	173mm (6.75in.)	173mm (6.75in)

*Aerial in folded position.

(later MG-34) machine-gun, on a pedestal mounting protected by a light armoured shield 8mm thick, capable of high elevation to fulfil anti-aircraft requirements.

Popularly referred to as 'Badewannen' (bath-tubs) on account of their characteristic shape, both vehicles also often had their long designations shortened by the troops to 'Adler Panzerspähwagen'.

But as it turned out, their 8mm armour was insufficient to withstand contemporary small-arms fire, their cross-country ability was poor, and their centre of gravity was too high.

Although classified obsolete at the outbreak of the Second World War, these vehicles were used extensively during the Polish campaign and even saw service with infantry units in Russia owing to the shortage of armoured cars of more recent design. They were eventually relegated to a training role, however—issued to the heavy companies of the reconnaissance battalions of infantry divisions—and were replaced by a new series of four-wheeled armoured cars based on the standard Chassis I for the heavy passenger car.

Engine
Make: Adler, 6S (petrol). Some cars had a BMW engine, but sources referring to use of the Horch 6-cylinder engine are erroneous.
No. of cylinders: 6 (in-line).
Output: 60hp at 3200rpm.
Swept volume: 2916cc.
Cooling: Water, pump actuated.
Carburettor: One Solex.
Transmission
Gearbox: Crash type, giving four forward speeds and one reverse.
Drive: Rear axle only.
Clutch: Single dry plate.
Steering: Worm and sector device operating on front axle only.
Brakes: Hydraulic foot-brake acting on all four wheels; hand-brake acting on the transmission.
Chassis: Conventional commercial car chassis (frame type).
Suspension: All four wheels sprung by rigid, semi-elliptic springs. Tyres: 6.50 x 18 or 7.00 x 20 pneumatic, bullet-proof.
Armour: Flat face-hardened armour steel, welded, proof against small-calibre bullets beyond 25 metres. All surfaces 8mm thick with the exception of the floor, which was 5mm thick.
Armament: One 7.92mm MG-13 or MG-34 machine-gun on pedestal on Kfz.13. None on Kfz.14.
Ammunition: 2000 rounds of 7.92mm.
Performance (both models)
Maximum speed, road: 60kph (38mph).
Fuel capacity: 70 litres (15.4 galls).
Range, road: 320km (200 miles).
Range, cross-country: 230km (145 miles).
Turning circle diameter: 15m (49.2ft).
Trench crossing ability: 1m (3.28ft).
Grade ability: 15°.
Wading depth: 500mm (1.64ft).

2. Leichter Panzerspähwagen mit Einheitsfahrgestell I für Schwerer Personenkraftwagen Auto Union (light armoured reconnaissance car with the Standard Chassis I for Heavy Car) 4 x 4 Horch (Sd.Kfz.221 series)

During 1936-7 came the adoption of the range of standard Einheits chassis developed for the Wehrmacht for all forms of wheeled vehicle—armoured and unarmoured—taken into service with the German Army. Within the range were two chassis for the heavy passenger car: Einheitsfahrgestell I für Schwerer Personenkraftwagen (Standard Chassis I for Heavy Passenger Car); and Einheitsfahrgestell II für Schwerer Personenkraftwagen (Standard Chassis II for Heavy Passenger Car).

Standard Chassis I, developed for armoured cars, had a rear-mounted engine; and Chassis II had a front-mounted engine and was utilised for conventional military car bodies.

Development work on the standard chassis had commenced during 1934; and for the first time, great emphasis had been placed on the design of vehicles from technical as well as operational considerations. They now had to satisfy the following requirements:
1. Great reliability, insensitivity to defects during normal service use, and the ability to employ various grades of fuel.
2. Extensive economisation.
3. Simple construction, ease of replacement of damaged parts, ability to be repaired by semi-skilled personnel, and extensive standardisation.
4. Cross-country ability incorporating: good starting ability (powerful engine, adequate gearbox and differential gear), differential lock, running gear with limited rolling resistance, two axles with double tyres, in the case of six-wheeled vehicles, and good suspension; good grade ability (thereby preventing the driven front wheels from receiving too small a weight contribution when driving up-hill); high ground and belly clearance, with wheels well dispersed; good turning ability (4-wheel steering), the turning circle diameter to be from 1 to 3 metres plus two vehicle widths; good braking ability; low weight; limited ground pressure (achieved through low tyre pressures, use of multiple chassis construction and large wheels providing a greater bearing surface).

The demands were so great that the use of commercially available chassis or simple modifications of them proved to be impossible. Therefore, taking into account all the factors, a series of cargo and passenger-carrying vehicles was developed by the German automobile industry in conjunction with the Heereswaffenamt—and all the demands were admirably fulfilled. Of the many prototypes completed, the best models were exhibited at the 1936 automobile show in Berlin.

Full use was made of all the latest design and engineering techniques associated with vehicle technology, and it was hoped that standardisation and type minimisation would achieve simplification of manufacture and ease of maintenance and repair. (In practice, however,

the opposite situation arose.) Common features of all the vehicles were:
1. All-wheel drive.
2. Single tyres on all wheels.
3. Fully independent suspension.
4. Mounting of the stub-axles in rubber bearings.
5. Common drive to the front and rear axles.
6. Divided track rods.

Standard Chassis I for Heavy Passenger Car

The heavy cross-country Wehrmacht personnel carrier chassis I was different from the other standard models in that its engine was mounted at the rear. The radiator was very large and was located forward of the engine in the body. The length of the engine was minimised so that, despite its rear-mounting, an angle of departure of 40° was achieved. The angle of approach exceeded 60°. The steering wheel—located on the left-hand side —was inverted to accommodate the armoured body, which in turn provided the driver with excellent vision over the road. The basic chassis weighed about 1800kg (1.8 tons).

The first model, built by Auto-Union/Horch from 1935-40, was the type EG 1. This chassis was powered by a Horch 3.5-litre 8-cylinder V-type engine, developing 75hp at 3600rpm, and it had mechanical brakes. Armoured cars built on it were designated Leichter Panzerspähwagen Ausführung A (Light armoured car, Model A). An improved version, the Ausf.V, was built from 1940 until 1943. It was powered by a 3.8-litre Horch V8 engine developing 81hp at 3600rpm (after 1940 an uprated engine developing 90hp at 3600rpm was used) and had hydraulic brakes. Armoured cars built on this chassis were designated Leichter Panzerspähwagen Ausführung B (Light armoured car, Model B).

The chassis had four-wheel-drive, and there was a torque-converter having a limited differential action to prevent winding-up in the transmission. There was no auxiliary gearbox—the front axle being driven directly from the main gearbox, which incorporated a third differential. The transmission contained five gear ratios for forward motion and one for reverse, and an auxiliary low gear was provided for cross-country work. Apart from improving the tractive effort, the use of four-wheel drive increased obstacle-surmounting ability. A self-locking differential of the Rheinmetall pattern was used on the rear axle, with a normal differential on the front axle. (In some of the earlier models, the differential was of the ZF cam-and-plunger self-locking type.) The differential enabled all wheels on each side to receive driving power irrespective of the terrain.

In order to stabilise the loadings on the vehicle and to increase cross-country performance, fully independent suspension was employed on all four wheels. Each wheel was located by two radius arms of unequal length, sprung by two coil springs that were side by side and that operated between the lower arm and two brackets welded to the chassis frame. The drive passed between the two coil springs. Rubber buffers limited the deflection, and double-acting shock-absorbers were employed to prevent damage to the steerable wheels. This system provided considerable freedom of movement in soft soil. Detachable pressed steel wheels of six-stud pattern were used with 210 x 18 bullet-proof pneumatic tyres. The spare wheel was mounted outside the hull, on the off-side.

The chassis was provided with optional four-wheel steering. A control lever on the right of the driver operated a dog-clutch on the cross-shaft that engaged the rear-wheel steering. It was found later, however, that with small turns at speed the vehicle slewed to one side. For this reason, the four-wheel steering facility was not often used. Later it was forbidden for four-wheel steering to be used at speeds in excess of 20kph (13mph); and it was done away with completely in the Type 40 chassis.

This chassis, as with the other Einheits vehicles, was not altogether technically satisfactory. Its design was complex by virtue of its requirements, and it was therefore difficult to build. Consequently, deficiencies and malfunctions could not be corrected during production without losing a certain degree of standardisation.

Other features common to all models

The hulls were constructed of flat armour plates welded together. Where a turret was fitted, welded construction and flat plates were employed as for the hull. The turret was rotated from the gun-mounting and was mounted at four points, each consisting of a pair of ball-races acting as rollers. There was a fixed vision slit in each side of the turret.

The driver was usually provided with a single rectangular slit visor in the front plate, hinged at the top and opening outwards. Further visors were situated in both the rear and off-side front plates. Access to the fighting compartment was facilitated by a large door in each hull side-plate, hung on two hinges at the rear and opened by a handle from the inside and by a squared key from the outside.

Development history of light armoured cars (leichter Panzerspähwagen) based on Standard Chassis I for Heavy Passenger Car

The armoured cars developed on the standard chassis I were intended as replacements for the Kfz.13 and Kfz.14, and the Heereswaffenamt laid down specifications for two types of vehicle:
1. A weapons vehicle (Waffenwagen) with one machine-gun in a light open-topped rotating turret. [Later, this was amended to a requirement for a two-man turret mounting a 20mm KwK and a coaxial machine-gun.]
2. A radio vehicle (Funkwagen) with one machine-gun and 5-watt radio equipment.

Parent firm for the series was Eisenwerk Weserhütte AG in Bad Oeynhausen, the chassis being produced at the Horch-Werke of Auto-Union AG in Zwickau and assembly of the vehicle being carried out by F. Schichau of Elbing and Maschinenfabrik Niedersachsen of Hannover-Linden.

Beginning in 1937, these models were officially adopted:
1. Leichter Panzerspähwagen (MG) (Sd.Kfz.221).
2. Leichter Panzerspähwagen (Sd.Kfz.221) mit 2.8cm s.Pz.B.41.

	Model A Chassis (1936-8)	Model B Chassis (1939-42)
Weight of chassis:	1965kg (1.97 tons)	1965kg (1.97 tons)
Length of chassis:	4800mm (15.71ft)	4800mm (15.71ft)
Width of chassis:	1950mm (6.40ft)	1950mm (6.40ft)
Ground clearance:	240-245mm (9.5-9.7in)	240-245mm (9.5-9.7in)
Track (front and rear)	1646mm (5.40ft)[1]	1646mm (5.40ft)[1]
Wheelbase:	2800mm (9.18ft)	2800mm (9.18ft)
Wheel Width:	190mm (7.5in)	190mm (7.5in)
Engine		
Make:	Horch/Auto-Union	Horch/Auto-Union
Model:	V8-108 petrol (rear-mounted)	V8-108 petrol (rear-mounted)
No. of cylinders:	8 (66 deg.V)	8 (66 deg.V)
Output:	75hp at 3600rpm	81hp at 3600rpm[2]
Swept volume:	3517cc	3823cc
Cooling:	Water (pump)	Water (pump)
Carburettor:	2 x Solex 32 JFP	1 x Solex 30 JFP

Transmission:

Gearbox: Crash type, five forward and one reverse; chassis having differing ranges.

Drive: All four wheels. From gearbox, output shaft passed to front and rear differentials. Rear differential was integral with gearbox on Model A, separate on Model B.

Clutch: Single dry plate.

Steering: Four-wheel worm and sector steering device, rear-wheel steering disengagable. Steering wheel at 90° inclination.

Brakes:	Footbrake mechanical (cable-operated) acting on all four wheels.	Footbrake hydraulic acting on all four wheels.

Chassis: Box-shaped frame.

Suspension: All wheels were fully independently sprung, having double control arms and two side-by-side spiral springs per wheel. Detachable three-piece steel wheels with 210 x 18 low-pressure, bullet-proof, cross-country tyres.

Performance:

Fuel capacity:	100-110 litres (22-24 gallons)	100-110 litres (22-24 gallons)
Turning circle diameter		
front wheels only:	15m (49ft)	15m (49ft)
all wheels:	9.5m (31ft)	9.5m (31ft)
Grade ability:	19°-22°	19°-22°
Wading depth:	600mm (2ft)	600mm (2ft)
Vertical step:	250mm (10in)	250mm (10in)

1. Some cars were based on the short-track model, track measuring 1610mm (5.29ft) front and rear.
2. After 1940, the engine used was the 90hp at 3600rpm, together with two Solex 32 I.F.T.T. carburettors.

3. Leichter Panzerspähwagen (Sd.Kfz.221) mit Pz.B.39.
4. Leichter Panzerspähwagen (2cm) (Sd.Kfz.222).
5. Leichter Panzerspähwagen (Fu) (Sd.Kfz.223).
6. Kleiner Panzerfunkwagen (Sd.Kfz.260).
7. Kleiner Panzerfunkwagen (Sd.Kfz.261).

The overall weight of these cars was between 3.8 and 4.8 tons. Special open-hulled versions were used as driver training vehicles (Fahrschulfahreuge).

Although production ceased after 1942, many of these cars remained in service until the end of the war.

a. Leichter Panzerspähwagen (Le.Pz.Sp.Wg.) (MG) Sd.Kfz.221 mit Einheitsfahrgestell I für Schwerer Personenkraftwagen Ausführung A: light armoured reconnaissance vehicle (machine-gun) Sd.Kfz.221 with the Standard Chassis I for Heavy Passenger Car Model A

Motorised reconnaissance units received this vehicle as a replacement for the Kfz.13 armoured car from 1936. It was classed as a weapons vehicle (Waffenwagen). The Sd.Kfz.221 was often employed as a commander's car and, together with the various wireless cars, also formed mobile command posts and forward artillery observation posts. It was mainly deployed, however, in the reconnaissance company of the armoured reconnaissance battalion.

The two-man turret, which was open-topped, was in the form of a seven-sided truncated pyramid, with a wire-mesh anti-grenade screen over the front part only. It mounted only one 7.92 mm MG-34 machine-gun, protruding from the turret face, but an MP-38 or MP-40 machine-pistol was also carried. The MG-34 was capable of high elavation for defence against low-flying aircraft. No wireless equipment was carried, communication being by means of semaphore flags.

There were variations in the arrangement of the vision hatches in this model, but there was usually a single armour flap in the front of the driver's compartment. The vehicle was easily distinguishable from the other cars in this series by the inward-sloping glacis plate and the flat rear deck of the hull.

During 1941 the Pz.B.39 anti-tank rifle was mounted on this vehicle in addition to the standard MG-34 machine-gun, but only very few such conversions were carried out. Some cars were later rearmed with the 2cm s.Pz.B.41 tapered-bore light anti-tank gun (in which the bore tapered from 2.8cm at the breech to 2cm at the muzzle), which had a muzzle velocity of 4600fps. In such cases, the machine-gun was removed and the front of the open-topped turret was cut away to make room for the gun to be mounted above the turret-ring, which retained its normal shield. The sides of the turret were unaltered.

Characteristics (in addition to those of the Standard Chassis I Model A)
Weight, unladen: 3750kg (3.7 tons)
Weight, fully laden: 4000kg (4.0 tons).
Axle loading, front: 1500kg (1.5 tons).
Axle loading, rear: 2500kg (2.5 tons).
Crew: Two men (driver and commander/gunner).
Length, overall: 4800mm (14.71ft).
Width, overall: 1950mm (6.40ft).
Height over turret: 1700mm (5.56ft)
Height, over grenade mesh: 1800mm (5.90ft).
Armour
Type: Flat face-hardened armour steel, welded, proof against small calibre bullets at all ranges.
Hull: Nose, 14.5mm; glacis, 6mm; sides, 8mm; rear, 8mm; roof, 6mm; floor, 5mm.
Turret: Front, 8mm; sides, 5.5mm; rear, 5.5mm; roof, open.
Armament: One 7.92mm MG-34 machine-gun (later complemented by Pz.B.39 or replaced by s.Pz.B.41); one 9mm MP-38 or MP-40 machine-pistol; one 27mm signal pistol.
Turret
Traverse: 360° manual.
Elevation: —10° to +69°.
Ring diameter: 1450mm (57.0in).
Ammunition
7.92mm: 1200 rounds.
9mm: 350 rounds.
27mm signal cartridge: 12.
Stick grenades: 6.
Performance
Maximum speed, road: 80kph (50mph).
Maximum speed, cross-country: 40kph (25mph).
Radius of action, road: 320km (200 miles).
Radius of action, cross-country: 200km (125 miles).
Communication: No radio fitted; flag only.
Sighting and Vision: Open sight on machine-gun; usual armoured vision slits around hull and turret.

---

b. Leichter Panzerspähwagen (Le.Pz.Sp.Wg.) (2cm)

Sd.Kfz.222 mit Einheitsfahrgestell I für Schwerer Personenkraftwagen Ausführung A oder B: light armoured reconnaissance vehicle (20mm cannon) Sd.Kfz.222 with the Standard Chassis I for Heavy Passenger Car Model A or B

This was the standard armoured car introduced during 1938 as a weapons vehicle (Waffenwagen) for divisional reconnaissance units. It was built initially on the Model A chassis, but after 1938 the Model B chassis was employed. Remaining in service until the end of the war, the Sd.Kfz.222 proved very useful in North Africa and Western Europe. But it was found to be greatly restricted in Russia and was gradually replaced there by the Sd.Kfz.250/9 Leichter Panzerspähwagen (semi-tracked), which mounted the same turret. The Sd.Kfz.222 was built in much larger numbers than the Sd.Kfz.221 and was deployed mainly in the reconnaissance companies of tank battalions. The three-man crew consisted of a driver, a commander/gunner and a radio-operator. The radio equipment had a range of about 4½ miles.

The turret, which was extremely cramped despite being larger than that of the Sd.Kfz.221, was in the form of a shallow truncated ten-sided pyramid. A hinged wire-mesh anti-grenade screen was fitted over the open top. This divided along the centre-line of the vehicle and could be folded outwards from the turret to facilitate firing of the armament, which had proved extremely difficult with the screen closed. The screen was also used as a framework for camouflage.

The main armament comprised a 20mm Kwk 30 or Kwk 38 (the latter being an armoured-car version of the standard 20mm aircraft cannon). Both were fully-automatic weapons firing from a 10-shot magazine at a rate of 280rpm in the case of the Kwk 30 and 480rpm in the case of the Kwk 38. The guns could fire both armour-piercing and high-explosive ammunition. A coaxial 7.92mm MG-34 was fitted. With the MG-34 on the left, the armament was mounted on a central pillar incorporating the traverse and elevation gear and attached to the floor of the fighting compartment. Sighting was by telescope, and a pedal-operated firing mechanism was employed. Traverse and elevation were controlled by a single hand-wheel, and the elevation was such that the weapon could be used against aircraft. Concentric with the gun mounting, the turret was traversed from the mounting by means of a linking arm incorporating a spring shock-absorber. Two mechanically-fired smoke projectors were also fitted on each side of the turret.

The hull of this and later vehicles had the rear part of the fighting compartment stepped down and the engine deck more sharply sloped to give the driver greater field of view when reversing. This was impossible with the Sd.Kfz.221. Another deviation from the design of the Sd.Kfz.221 was that the upper nose-plate now widened instead of narrowed towards the front. On later models of the Sd.Kfz.222 and companion vehicles the thickness of the nose-plate was increased from 14.5mm to 30mm and double hinged flaps were provided for the driver. Vehicles based on the Model B chassis had more powerful engines.

On 20th April 1940 the Heereswaffenamt issued orders to Appel in Berlin-Spandau and Schichau in Elbing for the construction of a 2cm elevating mounting (Model 38) for the Sd.Kfz.222 to enable the vehicle to be used as an air-defence weapon. In this version, the overall weight was 5000kg (5 tons).

Characteristics (in addition to those of the Standard Chassis I Models A and B)
Weight, unladen: 4300kg (4.3 tons).
Weight, fully laden: 4800kg (4.8 tons).
Axle loading, front: 1850kg (1.85tons).
Axle loading, rear: 2950kg (2.95 tons).
Crew: Three men (driver, commander/gunner and radio-operator).
Length, overall: 4800mm (14.71ft).
Width, overall: 1950mm (6.40ft).
Height, overall: 2000mm (6.56ft, including grenade screen).
Armour
Type: Flat face-hardened armour steel, welded—originally proof agianst small calibre bullets and later also proof against light and anti-tank guns.
Hull: Nose, 14.5mm (later increased to 30mm); glacis, 6mm; sides, 8mm; rear, 8mm; roof, 6mm; floor, 5mm.
Turret: Front, 8mm (later increased to 10mm); sides, 8mm; rear, 8mm; roof, open.
Armament
One 20mm Kwk 30 or Kwk 38 L/55 cannon ⎫ coaxially
One 7.92mm MG-34 machine gun ⎬ mounted in
⎭ turret
One 9mm MP-38 or MP-40 machine-pistol.
One 27mm signal pistol (later supplemented by smoke dischargers).
Turret:
Traverse: 360°, manual.
Elevation: −4° to +87°.
Ring diameter: 1450mm (57.0in).
Ammunition
20mm: 220 rounds (100 AP, 120 HE).
7.92mm: 1100-2000 rounds.
27mm signal pistol cartridges (or smoke cannisters): 12.
Stick grenades: 6.
Performance
Maximum speed, road: 80kph (50mph).
Maximum speed, cross-country: 40kph (25mph).
Radius of action, road: 300km (187 miles).
Radius of action, cross-country: 180km (110 miles).
Communication: W/T (short-range), R/T intercom, flag.
Sighting and Vision: T.Z.F.3a telescopic sight and Fliegervisier (aircraft visor) 38 for anti-aircraft defence. Numerous vision slits around hull and turret with bullet-proof laminated glass blocks.

---

c. Leichter Panzerspähwagen (Le.Pz.Sp.Wg.) (Fu) Sd.Kfz.223 mit Einheitsfahrgestell I für Schwerer Personenkraftwagen Ausführung A oder B: light armoured reconnaissance vehicle (wireless) Sd.Kfz.223 with the Standard Chassis I for Heavy Passenger Car Model A or B
This was a wireless car (Funkwagen) model of the Sd.Kfz.222, introduced into service during 1938. It was specially developed to carry long-range radio equipment and was generally similar to the Sd.Kfz.222 but had a smaller turret mounting only a 7.62mm MG-34 machine-gun and a frame aerial around the hull. The restangular frame aerial was mounted on four supports and could be lowered when necessary to reduce the silhouette. But this aerial, which was a different pattern from that fitted to the heavier wireless cars, proved unsatisfactory and was eventually replaced by a vertical rod type. When lowered, the aerial fitted snugly around the hull.

In contrast to that of the Sd.Kfz.221 and the Sd.Kfz.-222, the turret was nine-sided. Like the others, however, it was open at the top and covered at the front by a hinged wire-mesh anti-grenade screen.

The vehicle was employed in the reconnaissance companies of armoured reconnaissance battalions. (Note: A French light armoured car was also designated Sd.Kfz.223 le.Pz.Sp.Wg.(f) and should not be confused with this vehicle.)

Characteristics (in addition to those of the Standard Chassis I Models A and B)
Weight, unladen: 3950kg (3.95 tons).
Weight, fully laden: 4400kg (4.40 tons).
Axle loadings, front: 1650 (1.65 tons).
Axle loadings, rear: 2750kg (2.75 tons).
Crew: Three men (driver, commander/gunner and radio-operator).
Length, overall: 4800mm (14.71ft).
Width, overall: 1950mm (6.40ft).
Height with aerial raised: 1830mm (6.0ft).
Height with aerial lowered: 1750mm (5.74ft).
Armour
Type: Flat face-hardened armour steel, welded—originally proof against small calibre bullets, and later also proof against light anti-tank guns.
Hull: Nose, 14.5mm (later increased to 30mm); glacis, 6mm; sides, 8mm; rear, 8mm; roof, 6mm; floor, 5mm.
Turret: Front, 8mm; sides, 5.5mm; rear, 5.5mm; roof, open.
Armament
One 7.92mm MG-34 machine-gun.
One 9mm MP-38 or MP-40 machine-pistol.
One 27mm signal pistol (later replaced by single smoke discharger on right-hand side of turret).
Turret
Traverse: 360°, manual.
Elevation: −10° to +69°.
Ring diameter: 1450mm (57.0in).
Ammunition
7.92mm: 1200 rounds.
9mm: 350 rounds.
27mm signal pistol cartridges (or smoke cannisters): 12.
Stick grenades: 6.
Performance
Maximum speed, road: 80kph (50mph).
Maximum speed, cross-country: 40kph (25mph).
Radius of action, road: 320km (200 miles).
Radius of action, cross-country: 200km (125 miles).

Communication: W/T (long-range), R/T intercom, flag.
Sighting and Vision: Open sight on machine-gun, usual armoured vision slits with bullet-proof laminated glass blocks around hull and turret.

d. Kleiner Panzerfunkwagen (Kl.Pz.Fu.Wg.) Sd.Kfz.260 mit Einheitsfahrgestell I für Schwere Personenkraftwagen Ausführung A oder B: light armoured wireless vehicle Sd.Kfz.260 with the Standard Chassis I for Heavy Passenger Car Model A or B

This small armoured wireless vehicle was employed by headquarters units for communicating with divisional or brigade headquarters, for which a much greater range was required from the wireless set. The most prominent differences from the Sd.Kfz.223 version were that the turret was set further to the rear of the hull to make room for the bulky wireless equipment and it very rarely mounted any armament. The open turret was often locked at 12 o'clock position and covered by a tarpaulin. A long rod-type aerial was employed, which was the only external feature that distinguished the Sd.Kfz.260 from the early models of the Sd.Kfz.261 light armoured wireless vehicle with their frame-type aerial. It was, however, impossible to distinguish it from the later model of the Sd.Kfz.261, which had a rod-aerial of the same type.

Characteristics (as for the Sd.Kfz.223 but with the following differences)
Weight, unladen: 3815kg (3.82 tons).
Weight, fully laden: 4300kg (4.30 tons).
Axle loadings, front: 1600kg (1.6 tons).
Axle loadings: rear: 2700kg (2.7 tons).
Crew: Four men (driver, commander, two wireless operators).
Length, overall: 4830mm (15.85ft).
Width, overall: 1990mm (6.54ft).
Height, without aerial: 1780mm (5.84ft)
Armament: Most often, none fitted; 9mm MP 38 or MP40 machine-pistol carried for close-in protection.
Turret: Locked at 12 o'clock.
Ammunition: 350 rounds of 9mm.
Communication: W/T (ultra-long-range), R/T intercom, flag.

e. Kleiner Panzerfunkwagen (Kl.Pz.Fu.Wg.) Sd.Kfz.261 mit Einheitsfahrgestell I für Schwerer Personenkraftwagen Ausführung A oder B: light armoured wireless vehicle Sd.Kfz.261 with the Standard Chassis I for Heavy Passenger Car Mode/ A or B

This vehicle was externally identical to the Sd.Kfz.260 except that the earlier production models had a folding-frame aerial. Because of the bulk of the radio equipment, no armament was carried. The folding frame aerial was of a similar type to that fitted on the Sd.Kfz.223 and it proved to be an encumberance under combat conditions. It was therefore replaced on later production models by a rod-type aerial of the type used on the Sd.Kfz.260.

Characteristics (as for the Sd.Kfz.260 but with the following differences)

Weight, unladen: 3855kg (3.86 tons).
Weight, fully laden: 4300kg (4.3 tons).
Radius of action, road: 310km (194 miles).
Radius of action, cross-country: 200km (133 miles).

3. Schwerer Geländegängiger Gepanzerter Personenkraftwagen (s.gl.gp.Pkw.) auf Einheitsfahrgestell II für Schwerer Personenkraftwagen, Sd.Kfz.247 (4-Rad): heavy cross-country armoured passenger car on the Standard Chassis II for heavy passenger car, Sd.Kfz.247 (4-wheeled)

In contrast to the previously described series, this model of the Sd.Kfz.247 was based on the Standard Chassis II for Heavy Passenger Car, which had the engine mounted at the front. The vehicle was not classified as an armoured reconnaissance vehicle but as an armoured personnel carrier. As far as is known, it was the only armoured vehicle produced on this chassis.

The Sd.Kfz.247 vehicle role was originally fulfilled by an earlier model, designated Sd.Kfz.247 (6-Rad), based on the chassis of the Krupp L2H 43 and L2H 143 six-wheeled lorries (see page 66). But as with most other military bodies, the standard chassis for the heavy passenger car later took over the role. Originally intended as an armoured reconnaissance vehicle, one was issued to each reconnaissance unit as a so-called standard vehicle prior to the war. Only about twenty were produced, and shortly after adoption by the Wehrmacht during 1939 they were primarily used as armoured cross-country staff-cars for high-ranking officers.

Parent firm for the vehicle was Daimler-Benz Werk AG, Werke Berlin-Marienfelde, and the armoured body was produced by Deutschen Edelstahl A. G., Werk Hannover-Linden. Two four-wheel-chassis models were adopted—Sd.Kfz.247/I and Sd.Kfz.247/II—and they differed only in the type of wireless equipment carried and in minor alteration to the front of the hull.

The vehicle utilised the Auto-Union/Horch Ia chassis with four-wheel steering, which—apart from the location of the engine—was automotively indentical to the Standard Chassis I for Heavy Passenger Car already described.

Characteristics
Weight, unladen: 3700kg (3.70 tons).
Weight, fully laden: 4460kg (4.46 tons).
Axle loadings, front: 2260kg (2.26 tons).
Axle loadings, rear: 2200kg (2.20 tons).
Crew: Six men (driver and five passengers).
Length, overall: 5000mm (16.40ft).
Width, overall: 2000mm (6.56ft).
Height, overall: 1800mm (5.90ft).
Ground clearance: 230mm (9.05in).
Track, front and rear: 1646mm (5.40ft).
Wheelbase: 3000mm (9.84ft).
Wheel width: 190mm (7.5in).
Engine
Make: Horch/Auto-Union.

Model: V8-108 petrol.
No. of cylinders: 8 (66°V).
Output: 81hp at 3600rpm.
Swept volume: 3823cc.
Cooling: Water (pump).
Carburettor: 2 x Solex 30 BFH.
Transmission
Gearbox: Crash type, giving five forward speeds and one reverse speed.
Drive: Two differentials, one per axle, giving all-wheel drive.
Clutch: Single dry plate.
Steering: Four-wheel worm and sector steering device, rear wheel steering disengagable. Steering wheel in line with steering column, at right-angles to normal position.
Brakes: Hydraulic footbrake acting on all four wheels; handbrake acting on rear wheels only.
Chassis: Box-shaped frame.
Suspension: Double control arm, two spiral springs per wheel each. All wheels fully independently sprung. Detachable steel three-piece wheels with 210 x 18 low-pressure, bullet-proof cross-country tyres.
Armour
Type: Flat face-hardened armour steel, welded, proof against small-calibre bullets at all ranges.
Hull: Nose, 8mm; glacis, 6mm; sides, 6mm; rear, 6mm; roof, open; floor, 5mm.
Turret: None fitted.
Armament: Only personal weapons of crew.
Ammunition: Optional.
Performance
Maximum speed, road: 80kph (50mph).
Maximum speed, cross-country: 40kph (25mph).
Fuel capacity: 160 litres (35 gallons).
Range, road: 450km (280 miles).
Range, cross-country: 320km (200 miles).
Turning circle diameter, front wheel steering only: 13.5m (44ft).
Turning circle diameter, all-wheel steering: 9m (29ft).
Trench crossing ability: 1m (3.28ft.).
Grade ability: 21°.
Vertical step: 200mm (8in).
Wading depth: 600mm (2ft).
Communication: Model I and II had different radio-equipment, both long-range. Normal R/T intercom was installed.
Sighting and Vision: Conventional armoured visors with laminated bullet-proof glass blocks.

---

4. Experimental Four-wheeled Armoured Cars

---

a. Mittlerer Panzerspähwagen (m.Pz.Sp.Wg.) Vs.Kfz.231 (4-Rad): medium armoured reconnaissance vehicle (experimental) Vs.Kfz.231 (4-wheeled)

During 1941 the Heereswaffenamt (Wa.Prüf.6) was ordered to develop a new standard four-wheeled armoured car. On 21st July 1941 a specification was issued for a light-weight four-wheeled version of the eight-wheeled Sd.Kfz.231 GS armoured car. This vehicle was to utilise all the major components of the parent vehicle with

the exception of the engine, gearbox and suspension. An air-cooled six-cylinder Tatra diesel engine developing 125hp was specified, and this was to be mounted inside the shortened engine compartment of the GS vehicle. The seven-ton car was thus to achieve a speed of 85kph. The face-hardened armour was to be up to 30mm thick on the front, and the remaining surfaces were to vary between 8mm and 14.5mm.

Parent firm for the vehicle was Büssing-NAG in Berlin-Oberschönweide, and assembly was to have been carried out by Horch of Zwickau. The crew was to consist of four men and the armament—originally specified as a 2cm KwK 39/1—was later amended to a 5cm KwK 39/1, mounted in a fully-rotating turret, coaxial with a 7.62mm MG-42. One thousand of these cars were actually ordered with a date of October 1943 for the start of production. Experience in Russia, however, showed that the light reconnaissance vehicle would be more valuable as a tracked vehicle, with the result that the Sd.Kfz.250 Caesar semi-tracked armoured car was adopted instead.

b. Amphibious Schildkröte (turtle) armoured car series developed by Hans Trippel

During the period 1941 to 1944, Hans Trippel of the Trippelwerke at Molsheim (a firm long associated with amphibious cars) was concerned with the development of a series of armoured amphibious reconnaissance vehicles as a private venture.

Trippel experienced much difficulty in obtaining first the necessary priorities to start production and then the components to which they applied. But it appears (since there was a vehicle designated S.G.6) that at least six prototypes were finally constructed, each differing from the others in some way or another. These were either unsuccessful during their trials or were not required by the army, for quantity production was never begun.

Initially, a series of three small vehicles called Schildkröte (turtle) was developed, based on the S.G.6 amphibious staff car—one of several that had been developed earlier. Hans Trippel proposed the idea to the Heereswaffenamt during 1941, and an order for one prototype was placed in January 1942. This vehicle was known as the Schildkröte I.

Basically the first model was an S.G.6 chassis with a standard six-cylinder Opel 2.5-litre engine, standard front and rear suspension, standard steering system and 7mm to 7.5mm armour. Additional components not normally identified with the S.G.6 were an Opel 2.5-litre gearbox and a new (F.2) transfer box. The armament consisted of only one 7.92mm MG-81 machine-gun, and a searchlight was mounted on the turret. An unsuccessful demonstration of this vehicle took place before army authorities in Berlin during the latter half of March 1942, upon which the design was cancelled and development of a second version was requested. An order for two further vehicles was placed with Trippelwerke on 14th April 1942.

The mechanical components and layout of the Schildkröte II were the same as those for the Schildkröte I except for the steering gear, of which a special type was developed. The armour basis was increased to 10mm. An experiment with paddle (bladed wheel) water propulsion proved unsuccessful and the idea was abandoned in favour of propeller drive.

The Schildkröte II was unsuccessfully demonstrated first before Field Marshal Milch and his staff on 1st and 2nd May 1942 and then officially in Berlin in June 1942. The vehicle demonstrated was without a turret, although it was intended to mount an open-topped octagonal turret with a 20mm MG-151/20 or a 7.92mm MG-81 with a coaxial 7.92mm MG-34. The guns were electrically fired, and hand traverse and elevation of the turret and mounting was provided. The MG-151 mounting incorporated a ring-spring buffer. Ammunition for this weapon was stowed in steel boxes measuring 151mm x 400mm x 650mm.

Work on the third and final Schilkröte model (Schild kröte III) was started in June 1942 and the vehicle was demonstrated in Berlin on 1st October 1942. Its main distinguishing features were the single MG-151 turret-mounting and the use of a 75hp Tatra engine. The armour basis was the same as for the Schildkröte II except that the front was increased to 14.5mm. The turret was mounted centrally on the hull roof-plate—the driver sitting forward of the fighting compartment in the centre of the hull—and the engine was mounted at the rear. But like its predecessors, this vehicle was rejected.

During 1943 Trippel continued development of a similar series of 'E' (Einheits) amphibious armoured cars, about which little is known. There was an E.3 model, having a fully-rotating turret mounting a small gun, and the E.3M Munitionstransportwagen—basically the same vehicle but without a turret and open-topped. Prototypes of these vehicles were completed during 1944. Based on the S.G.7. amphibious staff car, they had rear-mounted Tatra air-cooled V-8 diesel engines and faceted armour. They were tested by the Wehrmacht in October 1944, but no production ensued.

Characteristics	Schildkröte I	Schildkröte II	Schildkröte III
Weight, unladen:	1500kg (1.5 tons)	2100kg (2.1 tons)	2658kg (2.7 tons)
Weight, fully laden:	1750kg (1.8 tons)	2350kg (2.4 tons)	2900kg (2.9 tons)
Crew:	Two men—driver in hull, gunner in turret.		
Length, overall:	4460mm (14.64ft)	4460 mm (14.64ft)	4860mm (15.92ft)
Width, overall:	1751mm (5.58ft)	1751mm (5.58ft)	1900mm (6.23ft)
Height, overall:	1560mm (5.12ft)	1560mm (5.12ft)	1400mm (4.59ft) *
Ground clearance:	254mm (10in)	254mm (10in)	254mm (10in)
Track, front and rear:	1750mm (5.75ft)	1750mm (5.75ft)	1450mm (4.76ft)
Wheelbase:	2800mm (9.18ft)	2800mm (9.18ft)	2500mm (8.20ft)
Wheel width:	190mm (7.5in)	190mm (7.5in)	190mm (7.5in)
Engine			
Make:	Opel	Opel	Tatra**
Model:	OHV	OHV	M.87
No. of cylinders:	6	6	8
Output:	54bhp at 3600rpm	54bhp at 3600rpm	75bhp at 3800rpm
Swept volume:	2500cc	2500cc	3600cc
Cooling: Water; two independent systems, two radiators. Pump circulation.			Air
Carburettor:	2 x Solex	2 x Solex	2 x Solex

Transmission (I, II and III)	
Gearbox:	Opel crash type, giving four forward speeds and one reverse speed; additional high/low two-speed Z.F. transfer box.
Drive, land:	Two self-locking differentials—one per axle—giving all-wheel drive.
Drive, water	Single propeller engaged by control in driver's compartment, giving one forward and one reverse speed.
Clutch:	Single dry plate.
Steering	(land) Trippel worm and sector type; (water) rudder***.
Brakes	Hydraulic footbrake, mechanical handbrake—both acting on all four wheels.
Chassis	Box-shaped frame.
Suspension	Independent parallel-link type with spiral springs and hydraulic shock-absorbers. Disc wheels with Continental 6.00 x 18 low-pressure, bullet-proof, cross-country tyres.

Armour
Type: Flat rolled plate, welded, except for two bent plates forming part of each wheel casing.

	Schildkröte I	Schildkröte II	Schildkröte III
Hull:	5.5mm—7.5mm	5.5mm—10mm	5.5mm—14.5mm
Turret:	7mm	10mm	10mm
Armament	One 7.92mm MG-81	20mm MG-151/20 or one 7.92mm MG-18 and coaxial 7.92mm MG-34	One 20mm MG-151

Notes:
* Without turret, turret not fitted. ** Originally propelled by air-cooled Phanomen 27 engine. *** Schildkröte II had a new steering gear.

Performance (I, II and III)			Fuel capacity:	70 litres (15.5 gallons)
Maximum speed, land:	80kph (50mph)		Range, road:	240km (150 miles)
Maximum speed, water:	4.9mph to 5.5mph at 1500rpm		Range, water:	107km (67 miles)
Turret (I, II and III)				
Traverse:	360° (manual)			

18. Mittlerer Gepanzerter Personen-kraftwagen Adler Kfz.13 'Waffen-wagen' or 'Badewanne'.
19. Kfz.13 during manoeuvres.
20. Kfz.13, in the foreground, during manoeuvres. The vehicle in the centre is the radio version, Kfz.14.

▲ 18

▲ 19   20 ▼

21. Kfz.13s forming part of a reconnaissance group during manoeuvres. The three leading vehicles are Sd.Kfz.232 6-wheeled armoured cars.
22-24. Kfz.13s taking part in operations.

▲ 21

22 ▼

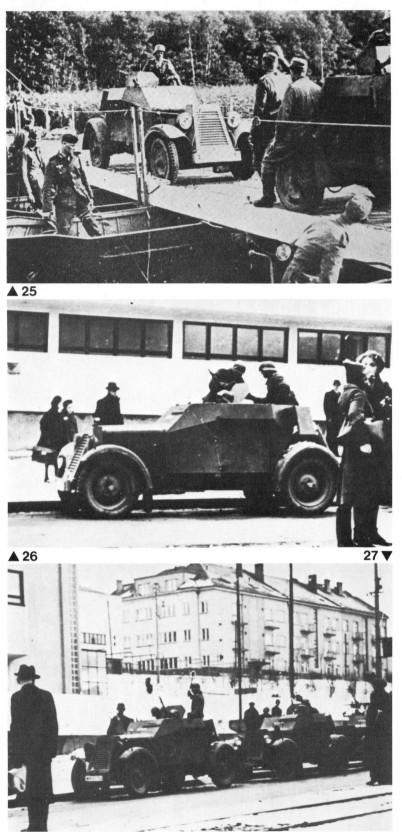

25-27 Kfz.13s taking part in operations.
28. Mittlerer Gepanzerter Funkraftwagen Adler Kfz.14.
29. Kfz.14 taking part in an exercise.
30. A Kfz.14, on the extreme left, with two Kfz.13s.

▲ 25

▲ 26   27 ▼

▲ 28

▲ 29   30 ▼

33

31. The standard chassis I for heavy passenger car with steel body being tested at the Auto-Union proving grounds.

32. The basic standard chassis I, showing the rear-mounted engine.

33. Leichter Panzerspähwagen Sd.Kfz.221 — the first of the armoured reconnaissance cars based on the standard chassis I for the heavy passenger car.

34, 35. Leichter Panzerspähwagen Sd.Kfz.221.

▲ 31

▲ 32   33 ▼

▲34

35▼

36-39. Leichter Panzerspähwagen Sd.Kfz.221.
40. The foremost vehicle is an Sd.Kfz.221. Behind it are an Sd.Kfz.222 and an Sd.Kfz.260.

▲ 36

▲ 37

38 ▼

41. A propaganda photograph of an Sd.Kfz.221 on the French coast — allegedly 'looking towards Dover' — interesting since it shows the wire-mesh surround on the top of the rear deck, which enabled the mounting of the turret and protected the crew from hand-grenades. Successive models had slight modifications to the rear armour.
42, 43. Further views of the Sd.Kfz.221.
44. Sd.Kfz.221s being refuelled from a bowser.

▲41   42▼

45. Sd.Kfz.221 armoured cars in Tripoli during May 1941.

46. An Sd.Kfz.221 operating along-side an Sd.Kfz.232 6-wheeled armoured car.

47. One of the Sd.Kfz.221 vehicles sold to China.

48. An Sd.Kfz.221 fitted with the 2cm sPz B41 tapered-bore anti-tank gun. An interesting alteration is the cut-away front turret. This view shows a vehicle without the wire-mesh grenade screens over the turret.

▲49

▲50   51▼

49. Another view of the sPz B41 conversion of the Sd.Kfz.221. Here the wire-mesh grenade screens have been fitted, but due to the alteration of the turret they differ somewhat from those of the parent vehicle.

50. Early production model of the Leichter Panzerspähwagen Sd.Kfz.222 'Waffenwagen'.

51. One of the characteristic visual features of the early model Sd.Kfz.222 was the symmetry of the frontal vision flaps. As is indicated here, all four vision flaps on the frontal section of the hull were identical.

52. Another important visual difference was the site of the armoured flaps around the turret. Here can be seen the original arrangement on the early Sd.Kfz.222.

53. The remaining major visual difference was the omission of armour protection on the air-intake grille at the rear, shown here.

▲ 54

54. The early Sd.Kfz.222 took part in all of the early operations. Here it is seen in the campaigns against the Low Countries.
55. Early Sd.Kfz.222 models in action with the Afrika Korps.
56. Early Sd.Kfz.222s in Norway.
57. A mixture of German armoured cars taking part in a parade. The two vehicles in the foreground are early Sd.Kfz.222s.
58. As with the Sd.Kfz.221, several Sd.Kfz.222 armoured cars were exported to China. It is interesting to note here the diversity of armament with which the Chinese fitted these vehicles.

▲ 55   56 ▼

▲ 57

58 ▼

59. Later version of the Sd.Kfz.222.

60. As can be seen, the two vision ports on the driver's side of the hull were still hinged but had been slightly altered.

61. The other two hull vision ports at the front were now fixed and markedly different in shape.

62. The turret vision flaps had also been changed but the most noticeable visual difference was at the rear. The air-intake louvres were now protected by a wedge-shaped armoured box.

▲61

62▼

▲63

▲64

65 ▼

63. A bird's-eye view showing the mounting of the 2cm weapon in the turret and also the restricted space.

64. Clearly seen here is the arrangement of the grenade screens on the turret as well as the coil spring suspension.

65. The later production model of the Sd.Kfz.222 dispensed with the triangular hub-plates on the wheels.

66. A special tarpaulin was often used to cover the open turret — particularly when the vehicle was not taking part in operations. This Sd.Kfz.222 is being loaded into a transport aircraft.

67. Due to the restricted space in the turret, the grenade screens were usually lowered only in street fighting or on patrols where ambush was possible at close quarters. Normally, the screens were raised so that the commander could sit atop the turret.

68. Much use was made of the later model Sd.Kfz.222 by the Afrika Korps.

69. These cars were often draped with camouflage nets against observation from the air.

70. The high-angle mounting for the armament enabled it to be used for anti-aircraft protection.

71. The le-Pz.Sp.Wg.(Fu) Sd.Kfz.223 armoured car was developed as a command/radio companion to the Sd.Kfz.222, with which it was identical but for its smaller turret and armament. The early version shown here was based on the early production Sd.Kfz.222 chassis.

▲ 68

▲ 69   70 ▼

▲72

▲73

74▼

52

72. Right-hand side of early production Sd.Kfz.223 with frame aerial raised.
73. With frame aerial lowered.
74. Left-hand side of early production Sd.Kfz.223 with frame aerial lowered.
75. Rear view of Sd.Kfz.223 showing the unarmoured radiator grille.
76. Early Sd.Kfz.223 in the field.

▲75

76▼

53

▲ 77

77. Early Sd.Kfz.223 in the field.
78. Early Sd.Kfz.223 with the Afrika Korps.
79. Early Sd.Kfz.223 in the Low Countries.
80. Sd.Kfz.223 taking part in a parade in Paris.
81. An Sd.Kfz.223 operating with a Kfz.12 'Waffenwagen' in Russia.
82. Rear view of Sd.Kfz.223 with aerial folded.

▲ 78   79 ▼

83. Early version of Sd.Kfz.223 in China.
84. Later production model of Sd.Kfz.223 with the new vision ports arrangement.
85. Rear view of the later Sd.Kfz.223 showing the armoured cowl over the radiator grille.
86. Kl.Pz.Fu.Wg. Sd.Kfz.260 armoured wireless car.
87. Very early version of Kl.Pz.Fu.Wg. Sd.Kfz.261 based on the Sd.Kfz.221 hull and chassis. Not many of these vehicles were built.
88. Early version of Sd.Kfz.261 in operation in Russia.

▲ 83

▲ 84

85 ▼

▲ 86

▲ 87

88 ▼

▲ 89

▲ 90   91 ▼

89. Later production model of Sd.Kfz.261 based on the early Sd.Kfz.222 hull and chassis.
90. Rear view of the same vehicle with aerial raised.
91. Final model of Sd.Kfz.261 based on later Sd.Kfz.222 hull and chassis.
92. The s.gl.gp.Pkw. Sd.Kfz.247/I (4 Rad) light armoured car.
93. The s.gl.gp.Pkw. Sd.Kfz.247/II (4 Rad) light armoured car, distinguishable from the Sd.Kfz.247/I by the frontal armoured shield and star aerial.

▲ 92   93 ▼

▲ 94

95 ▼

94. The standard chassis II for heavy passenger car, used as the basis for the Sd.Kfz.247 armoured car.

95-97. Prototype of Trippel armoured car in water.

98. Trippel E3M amphibian carrier.

▲ 96

▲ 97   98 ▼

▲ 99

99. Experiments were made with a radio-controlled 4-wheeled armoured lorry, intended as an ammunition carrier, but the vehicle was never developed.

100. Some improvised armoured cars — like these seen outside the Reichstag — were used for internal security duties.

101. An armoured version of the Volkswagen Kübel (Pkw. K1 Type 82) with a rotating turret mounting an MG-34. It had bulletproof glass and sand-filled tyres. Between 80 and 100 of these vehicles were produced, intended as replacements for the Kfz.13, and they were used mainly on the eastern front.

▲ 100   101 ▼

3. Six-wheeled vehicles

1. Schwerer Panzerspähwagen (heavy armoured reconnaissance car) 6 x 4 (Sd.Kfz.231 series)

This was the first tactical armoured car series to be adopted by the Wehrmacht, development of which began during the late twenties at the joint Soviet-German testing station at Kazan in Russia.

Since the eight- and ten-wheeled armoured car projects developed by Daimler-Benz Büssing-NAG and Magirus had proved too expensive, the Reichswehrministerium/Heereswaffenamt issued the same three firms with contracts for the development of armoured cars with similar characteristics but based on the commercial six-wheeled lorry chassis already in production. The specifications were for a six-wheeled armoured car model employing a 1.5-ton 6 x 4 cross-country lorry chassis.

Daimler-Benz had been experimenting during 1928 with their G-3 six-wheeled lorry, which was a further development of the earlier G-1 but with a markedly longer wheelbase. Eighty-nine were eventually built—four with an overall chassis length of 3200mm (10.50ft) and eighty-five with an overall chassis length of 3000mm (9.85ft). The aim was a multi-purpose chassis that would be reliable and safe, especially under the most unfavourable driving and road conditions; and the first prototype armoured car built on this chassis was designated G-3(p) (the 'p' standing for 'Panzer' or armoured). The chassis weighed 2200kg (2.2 tons) and was capable of supporting an armoured body weighing up to 2300kg (2.3 tons). The armoured body was produced by Deutschen-Werke A.G. in Kiel. A revolving turret mounting a single MG-13 7.92mm machine-gun was fitted, and the vehicle was powered by a 6-cylinder in-line water-cooled petrol engine (Model M 09) developing 60hp at 2800rpm. A standard sliding-pinion gearbox giving four forward speeds and one reverse speed was used—the drive being transmitted by way of a normal propeller shaft to the rear axles, each of which had its own differential. Dual controls—one at the front and

one at the rear—were provided with the steering wheels and they were inverted to allow better armour application. Larger tyres were employed to increase the cross-country performance.

This vehicle was delivered to the Heereswaffenamt for trials in 1929, when it was found that the front axle needed strengthening and that a larger radiator was necessary. Accordingly, the radiator area was increased by about 20%, together with the water capacity. It also became clear that the extremely long wheelbase of the G-3 model was a disadvantage, and adjustable tracks were tried on the rear wheels to increase cross-country performance.

During 1929, Daimler-Benz brought out their improved G-3a chassis. At this time, all chassis intended to be fitted with armoured bodies were provided with duplicate steering and produced in conformity with certain laid-down design standards while on the production line (see page 1). Work on the armoured car version began in 1930, and thirty-seven such cars—now designated G-3a(p)—were delivered to the Heereswaffenamt during 1932. The overall weight of each vehicle with the armoured body was 5000kg (5.0 tons), the chassis weight being 3260kg (3.26 tons). Again, the armoured bodies were produced by Deutschen-Werke A.G. in Kiel and the six-cylinder M 09 engine was employed but now uprated to 65hp at 2700rpm (and later to 68hp at 2900rpm). Only one 7.92mm machine-gun was mounted in the turret. The thirty-seven cars took part in the summer maneouvres of 1932, and the chassis remained in production until 1935.

In 1933 Büssing-NAG delivered their first model of the six-wheeled armoured car to the Wehrmacht. It was based on the Büssing G-31 lorry and was designated G-31(p). The early models of this car were powered by four-cylinder, in-line, Model G engines developing 60hp at 2500rpm, but later models had the Büssing six-cylinder engine developing 100hp at 3000rpm. These cars remained in production until 1935. Initially, twelve chassis were delivered, followed later by a further thirty-eight.

The final version of the six-wheeled armoured car was produced by Magirus (Klöckner-Humboldt-Deutz) during 1934, and it remained in service until 1936. Based on the Magirus 6 x 4 M-206 lorry, this car received the designation M-206(p). It was powered by the S 88 six-cylinder, in-line petrol engine developing 70hp at 2200rpm. One feature of this vehicle not shared by the other models was the use of bellying wheels on the central axle.

The six-wheeled armoured car, like the other models, was built as a reconnaissance model (Waffenwagen) and as a radio vehicle (Funkwagen). The Waffenwagen was designated s.Pz.Sp.Wg.Sd.Kfz.231 (6-Rad) and the Funkwagen was s.Pz.Sp.Wg.(Fu)Sd.Kfz.232 (6-Rad). There was also an additional heavy radio vehicle with a fixed turret, designated Panzerfunkwagen S.Kfz.263 (6-Rad). All of the previously mentioned firms produced models of the Waffenwagen—those by Daimler-Benz being armed with only a single 7.92mm MG-34, and those by Büssing-NAG and Magirus having coaxial mounting for a 20mm KwK 30 or 38 and a 7.92mm MG-34. The 20mm vehicles had a mounting for an anti-aircraft machine-gun on the turret roof. These vehicles—referred to by some wartime sources as ASP (often mis-construed as A5P)—were employed in the heavy platoons of motorised units.

Although most of the armoured bodies were produced by Deutschen-Werke A.G. in Kiel, some were also produced by Deutsche Edelstahlwerke in Hannover and were distinguishable by slight differences in the shape of the front radiator grilles. Owing to their relatively high weight and low engine output, these six-wheeled cars had relatively limited cross-country ability.

A total of 1000 of all models was produced up until 1936, when the various roles (Sd.Kfz.231, 232, 263) were taken over by the superior eight-wheeled GS chassis. Even so, some of the vehicles were used in France and Poland and were thereafter adopted for training purposes. British Intelligence has stated that there was an Sd.Kfz.233 version of this car (fixed 75mm KwK L/24 howitzer mounting), but nothing has come to light concerning such a vehicle.

The Basic Six-wheeled Chassis

Structurally, all of these vehicles were normal six-wheeled lorries with rigid axles sprung on longitudinal leaf springs.

The chassis frame was composed of pressed-steel V-section side-members and pressed-steel cross-members, and an auxiliary frame was provided to take the engine and gearbox. The individual joints were reinforced by means of butt straps.

Engines—mounted at the front of vehicles—varied according to the manufacturer, as did the clutch and gearbox (see page 67). But all vehicles had an additional direction-change gearbox, making available several speeds forward and in reverse. The drive was taken from the gearbox by way of universally-jointed shafts to the two rear axles, which had self-locking differentials. The front wheels were single and the rear wheels were double, and all were fitted with cross-country bullet-proof tyres. Suspension was by semi-elliptic springs: the front springs fitted to the frame with shock-absorbers and the rear wheels suspended by tubular transverse semi-elliptic springs.

Steering was on the front single axle only, but it could be accomplished from the front or rear of the vehicle. The front steering wheel was inclined at an angle of 90° to accommodate the sloping armoured body. The rear steering wheel, normally disengaged, was automatically engaged by the selection of reverse in the direction-change box. A duplicate set of main controls was provided for the rear driving position.

For improved cross-country performance, chains could be placed around the rear driving wheels and wide rims fitted inside the front wheels. The Magirus version had two bellying wheels forward of the rear wheel section. The method of braking varied according to the manufacturer (see page 67).

a. Schwerer Panzerspähwagen (s.Pz.Sp.Wg.) Sd.Kfz.231 mit Fahrgestell des Leichter Geländegängiger Lastkraftwagen (O): heavy armoured reconnaissance vehicle Sd.Kfz.231 with the chassis of the light cross-country lorry (commercial)

The Sd.Kfz.231 (6-Rad) was the weapons vehicle of the heavy platoons of the motorised units, basically according with the foregoing description.

b. Schwerer Panzerspähwagen (s.Pz.Sp.Wg.) (Fu) Sd. Kfz.232 mit Fahrgestell des Leichter Geländegängiger Lastkraftwagen (O); heavy armoured reconnaissance vehicle (wireless) Sd.Kfz.232 with the chassis of the light cross-country lorry (commercial)

This was the Funkwagen version of the six-wheeled armoured car fitted with a long-range 100-watt wireless set. It mounted a 2cm KwK 30 or 38 cannon and a coaxial 7.92mm MG-34 in the same type of turret as for the Sd.Kfz.231; but there was no anti-aircraft machine-gun mounting on the turret roof. A curved horizontal frame aerial consisting of parallel tubes was carried on two outriggers at the rear of the car, and it was characteristic of the wireless cars of the period. The frame had a central bearing that rested on an inverted 'U' turret support, allowing the turret to rotate beneath the aerial.

In other respects, this vehicle was identical to the Sd.Kfz.231 (6-Rad).

Characteristics (as for Sd.Kfz.231 but with the following differences)

Weight, unladen: 5500kg (5.5 tons).
Weight, fully laden: 6350kg (6.35 tons).
Length, overall: 5610mm (18.4ft).
Width, overall: 1850mm (6.06ft).
Height, excluding aerial: 2240mm (7.35ft).
Height, including aerial: 2900mm (9.5ft).
Range, road: 250km (150 miles).
Range, cross-country: 150km (95 miles).
Communication: W/T (long-range), R/T intercom, flag.
(Data given for vehicles based on the Magirus M-206(p) chassis).

c. Schwerer Panzerfunkwagen (s.Pz.Fu.Wg.) Sd.Kfz.263 mit Fahrgestell des Leichter Geländegängiger Lastkraftwagen (O): heavy armoured wireless vehicle with the chassis of the light cross-country lorry (commercial)

This was an armoured command vehicle similar in construction to the basic model but having a fixed turret, a large frame aerial similar but not identical to that fitted to the Sd.Kfz.232 and no anti-aircraft machine-gun mounting. The frame aerial was supported at four points and could be lowered if necessary. A long mast aerial could be deployed to enable the vehicle to act as a fixed field command post.

The space made available by the omission of the turret traverse gear enabled the stowage of the bulky long-range radio equipment.

Characteristics (as for Sd.Kfz.231, but with the following differences)
Weight, unladen: 5250kg (5.25 tons).
Weight, fully laden: 5800kg (5.8 tons).
Crew: Five men (two drivers and three crew members).
Height, excluding aerial: 2240mm (7.35ft).
Height, including aerial: 2930mm (9.6ft).
Armament: One 7.92mm MG-34 machine-gun.
Ammunition: 1500 rounds.
Communication: W/T (long-range), R/T intercom, flag.
(Data given for vehicle based on the Daimler-Benz G-3a(p) chassis.)

---

2. Schwerer Gepanzerter Personenkraftwagen (s.gp.Pkw) auf Fahrgestell des Leichter Geländegängiger Lastkraftwagen (O), Sd.Kfz.247 (6-Rad): heavy armoured personnel carrier on the chassis of the light cross-country lorry (commercial), Sd.Kfz.247 (6-wheeled)

This vehicle — the predecessor of the four-wheeled version based on the Standard Chassis II for the Heavy Passenger Car—utilised the chassis of the Krupp L2H 143 1.5-ton 6 x 4 lorry, Krupp Protze (Krupp limber). Apart from the six-wheeled armoured cars of the Sd.Kfz.231 series, it was the only six-wheeled armoured fighting vehicle to be employed by the Wehrmacht.

Its development began in 1936. The chassis was built by Krupp of Essen, and the armoured bodies were produced by Deutschen-Werke A.G. in Kiel. Only a few were manufactured before production ceased in 1938. Although originally developed as an armoured personnel carrier, the vehicle was often used as transportation for high-ranking officials and also as an artillery observation vehicle—in which role it incorporated the standard twin-periscope observation device.

The L2H 143 chassis, which was a modified version of the L2H 43, appeared in 1936. It was powered by an air-cooled four-cylinder Krupp M304 Boxer engine, mounted at the front, which allowed the use of a distinctive sloping bonnet on both the armoured and unarmoured versions. The engine was practically identical to that used in the Pz.Kpfw.I light tank. Both rear axles were driven, and their suspension was by the standard

Krupp coil-spring system. In other respects, the chassis layout was similar to that of the Sd.Kfz.231 (6-Rad) cars, but there was no facility for reverse steering.

Characteristics
Weight, unladen: 4600kg (4.6 tons).
Weight, fully laden: 5200kg (5.2 tons).
Crew: Six men.
Length, overall: 4600mm (15.1ft).
Width, overall: 1960mm (6.44ft).
Height, overall: 1700mm (5.57ft).
Ground clearance: 240mm (9.5in).
Track, front wheels: 1580mm (5.18ft).
Track, rear wheels: 1565mm (5.14ft).
Wheelbase: 2445+910mm (8.0+2.98ft).
Wheel width: 190mm (7.5in).
Engine
Make: Krupp.
Model: M304, petrol.
No. of cylinders: 4.
Output: 60hp at 2500rpm.
Swept volume: 3308cc.
Cooling: Air (compressor).
Carburettor: One Solex BFLH 40.
Transmission
Gearbox: Crash type, giving four speeds with transfer.
Drive: On both rear axles; two differentials, one per axle.
Clutch: Single dry plate.
Steering: Worm and sector steering device operating on front wheels only; no reverse steering facility.
Brakes: Hydraulic footbrake acting on all four wheels; handbrake acting on transmission.
Chassis: Box-shaped frame.
Suspension: Front wheels suspended on rigid, semi-elliptic leaf springs; two rear axles mutually interconnected, each having one spiral spring. Detachable steel three-piece wheels with 7.50 x 17 low-pressure, bullet-proof, cross-country tyres.
Armour
Hull: Nose, 8mm; glacis, 6mm; sides, 6mm; rear, 6mm; roof, open; floor, 5mm.
Turret: None fitted.
Armament: Only personal weapons of crew.
Ammunition: Optional.
Performance
Maximum speed, road: 70kph (44mph).
Maximum speed, cross-country: 35kph (22mph).
Fuel capacity: 110 litres (22 gallons).
Range, road: 390km (240 miles).
Range, cross-country: 270km (170 miles).
Turning circle diameter: 16m (53ft).
Trench crossing ability: 21°.
Vertical step: 200mm (8in).
Wading depth: 600mm (2ft).

---

3. Export Vehicles

One vehicle was produced by Krupp during 1936 for export to the Netherlands East Indies. This vehicle was based on the chassis of the L2H 143 lorry and was designed for internal security rather than reconnaissance.

Technical Characteristics for Basic 6-Wheeled Armoured Car Models in the Sd.Kfz.231 Range

Designation	G-3(p)	G-3a(p)	G-31(p)	M-206(p)
Manufacturer:	Daimler-Benz	Daimler-Benz	Büssing-NAG	Magirus
Weight, unladen:	4000kg (4.0 tons)	4850kg (4.85 tons)	5000kg (5.0 tons)	5300kg (5.3 tons)
Weight, fully laden:	5500kg (5.5 tons)	5700kg (5.7 tons)	5700kg (5.7 tons)	6000kg (6.0 tons)
Crew:	Four men	Four men	Four men	Four men
Length, overall:	5800mm (19.0ft)	5570mm (18.4ft)	5570mm (18.4ft)	5570mm (18.4ft)
Width, overall:	1820mm (5.97ft)	1820mm (5.97ft)	1820mm (5.97ft)	1820mm (5.97ft)
Height, overall:	2250mm (7.38ft)	2250mm (7.38ft)	2250mm (7.38ft)	2250mm (7.38ft)
Ground clearance:	265mm (10.4in)	225mm (8.9in)	225mm (8.9in)	240mm (9.5in)
Track, front wheels:	1600mm (5.25ft)	1600mm (5.25ft)	1550mm (5.09ft)	1695mm (5.55ft)
Track, inner rear:	1380mm (4.55ft)	1380mm (4.55ft)	1372mm (4.50ft)	1440mm (4.74ft)
Track, outer rear:	1820mm (5.97ft)	1820mm (5.97ft)	1812mm (5.95ft)	1840mm (6.04ft)
Wheelbase:	3200+950mm (10.5+3.12ft)	3000+950mm (9.84+3.12ft)	2715+950mm (8.90+3.12ft)	2500+950mm (8.20+3.12ft)
Wheel width:	170mm (6.7in)	I70mm (6.7in)	170mm (6.7in)	170mm (6.7in)
Engine				
Make:	Daimler-Benz	Daimler-Benz	Büssing NAG	Magirus
Model:	M 09 (petrol)	M 09 (petrol)	Type G (petrol)	S88 (petrol)
No. of cylinders:	6 (in-line)	6 (in-line)	4 (in-line)	6 (in-line)
Output:	60hp at 2800 rpm	65hp at 2900rpm	60hp at 2500rpm	70hp at 2200rpm
Swept volume:	3460cc	3663cc	3920cc	4562cc
Cooling:	Water (pump)	Water (pump)	Water (pump)	Water (pump)
Carburettor:	One Zenith	One Zenith	One Solex VFSL40	One Solex BFLH
Transmission	Constant mesh. Additional direction-change box making available both forward and reverse speeds.			
Gearbox:	Maybach DSG4 automatic vacuum gear-shift.			
Ratios:	Four-forward, one reverse	Five forward, four reverse	Six forward, six reverse	Four forward, four reverse
Drive:	On rear two axles (two inter-wheel and inter-axle differentials).			
Clutch:	Single dry plate	Multi dry plate	Single dry plate	Single dry plate
Steering	Screw or nut steering device; steering wheel at 90° inclination; additional steering controls at rear, but only front-wheel steering.			
Brakes				
Foot:	Hydraulic on six wheels	Hydraulic on six wheels	Hydraulic on six wheels	Mechanical on four wheels
Hand:	Mechanical on centre axle	Mechanical on centre axle	Mechanical on four wheels	Mechanical on transmission
Chassis	Box-shaped frame	Box-shaped frame	Box-shaped frame	Box-shaped frame
Suspension:	Semi-elliptic leaf springs, 8.27 x 18 cross country tyres, double at rear. Detachable three-piece pressed-steel wheels with cord-reinforced low-pressure bullet-proof tyres.			
Armour (all models)				
Type:	Flat face-hardened armour steel welded, proof against small calibre bullets at all ranges.			
Hull:	Nose, 14.5mm; glacis, 8mm; sides, 8 mm; rear, 8mm; roof 5mm; floor, 5mm.			
Turret:	Front, 14.5mm; sides, 8mm; rear, 8mm; roof, 5mm.			
Armament	7.92mm MG-34	7.92mm MG-34	2cm KwK 30 or 38 7.92mm MG-34 (Mounting for anti-aircraft machine-gun on turret roof)	2cm Kwk 30 or 38 7.92mm MG-34
Turret (all models)				
Traverse:	360°.			
Ammunition	7.92mm: 1500 rounds	7.92mm: 1500 rounds	2cm: 200 rounds 7.92mm: 1500 rounds	2cm: 200 rounds 7.92mm: 1500 rounds
Performance				
Maximum speed, road:	60kph (38mph)	Forward: 65kph (40mph) Reverse: 32kph (20mph)	Forward: 65kph (40mph) Reverse: 32kph (20mph)	Forward: 62kph (39mph) Reverse: 62kph (39mph)
Fuel capacity:	110 litres (22 gallons)	110 litres (22 gallons)	125 litres (28 gallons)	110 litres (22 gallons)
Range, road:	400km (250 miles)	250km (150 miles)	250km (150 miles)	300km (187 miles)
Range, cross-country:	250km (150 miles)	150km (94 miles)	200km (125 miles)	200km (125 miles)
Turning circle diameter:	19.5mm (64ft)	16.0m (52ft)	13.5m (44ft)	16.0m (52ft)
Grade ability:	13°	13°	20°	16°
Wading depth:	600mm (2ft)	600m (2ft)	600mm (2ft)	600mm (2ft)
Communication	W/T on some	W/T on some	W/T on some	W/T on some
Sighting and Vision	Open sight; normal vision-slits with glass blocks.		TZF 6 sight	TZF 6 sight

▲ 102

▲ 103   104 ▼

102. In 1928 Mercedes-Benz produced a cross-country chassis,
designated G3, for military use.
103. Another view of the G3 chassis
104. A special shortened version of
the G3 chassis, designated G3a.
This was used for a cross-country
lorry and, eventually, for a 6-wheeler
armoured car.
105. A 6-wheeled armoured car
chassis based on the G3a chassis.
106. The very early prototypes of the
6-wheeled armoured car were based
on the Mercedes-Benz G3 long-
wheelbase chassis. One of the
earliest, shown here, had a radiator
grille resembling that of the Kfz.13.
107. A later prototype had an
improved radiator grille, but it
retained the features of the earlier
prototypes.

▲105

▲106

107 ▼

108

108. Daimler-Benz produced the final prototypes of the 6-wheeled armoured car on the G3a chassis with shorter wheelbase.
109. A Daimler-Benz 6-wheeled armoured car prototype showing the rear steering wheel.
110-112. Daimler-Benz version of Sd.Kfz.231 (6 Rad) with single machine-gun mounting.

▲109   110▼

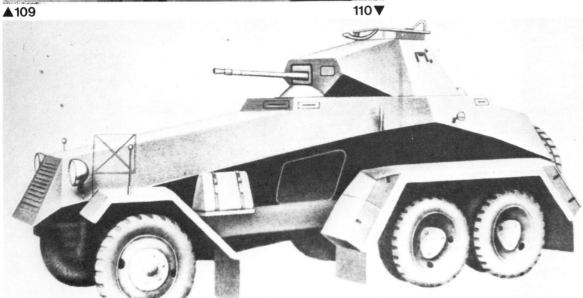

▲ 113

▲ 114

▲ 115

116 ▼

113. Three-quarters-front plan view of the Büssing-NAG version of the Sd.Kfz.231 (6 Rad), showing the coaxial arrangement of the turret machine-guns and also the MG-34 mounted alongside the driver.

114. The same vehicle ascending a bank. Note the spare wheel mounted at the extreme rear.

115. The Sd.Kfz.231 (6 Rad) in action. The turret is traversed to the offside, showing the armament arrangement.

116. The freedom of movement of the suspension when negotiating rough terrain is demonstrated here.

117. The same vehicle after negotiating the ditch.

118. The Sd.Kfz.231 (6 Rad) was sometimes fitted with an MG-34 in an anti-aircraft mounting, used as shown here.

119. An Sd.Kfz.231 (6 Rad) travelling in reverse, steered by the rear driver and with the turret traversed to face what is now the front. Noteworthy is the attachment of tracks around what are normally the rear wheels.

▲ 117

▲ 118

119 ▼

73

▲120

120. Later model of the Daimler-Benz version of the Sd.Kfz.231 (6 Rad) with modified radiator.
121-123. Later models of the Sd.Kfz.231 (6 Rad) with modified radiator and new armoured hull.
124. Early prototype of the Sd.Kfz.232 (Fu) (6 Rad).

WH–66049

▲121   **122▼**

▲125

▲126   127 ▼

Sd.Kfz.232 (6 Rad)
125. With coaxial armament, during a parade.
126. With the single 20mm MG.
127. With coaxial MG, in the field.
128. On an exercise, with the armament removed.
129. With modified radiator grille and coaxial armament. The driver's cowl and the radiator grille are open.
130. Taking part in a march-past before Hitler.
131. A side view that shows how the aerial was attached.

▲128

▲129

▼130

▼131

▲132   133▼

▼134   ▼135

132. Sd.Kfz.232 (6 Rad) armoured cars taking part in operations in Prague.

133. Sd.Kfz.232 (6 Rad) armoured cars of contrasting hull form. The radiator grille of the right-hand vehicle is rectangular, but that of the centre vehicle is a trapezium.

134. The s.Pz.Fu.Wg. Sd.Kfz.263 6-wheeled armoured radio car.

135. Rear view of the Sd.Kfz.263 (6 Rad).

136. Chassis of the Krupp L2H 143 on trials.

137. Chassis of the Krupp L2H 143 showing the main components.

138. The s.gl.Pkw. Sd.Kfz.247 (6 Rad).
139, 140. Sd.Kfz.247 (6 Rad) taking part in early parades in pre-war Germany.

▼138

139▼

140►

▲ **141.** Krupp 6-wheeled armoured car based on the L2H 143 lorry chassis, intended for export.

▼ **142.** A Krupp 6-wheeled armoured car being inspected by Prominenté.

4. Eight-wheeled vehicles

1. Schwerer Panzerspähwagen (heavy armoured reconnaissance car) 8 x 8 (Sd.Kfz.231 series)

The most powerful and best-known armoured car used by the Wehrmacht was undoubtedly the heavy eight-wheeler, of which there were several versions.

During 1934 the Heereswaffenamt issued Büssing-NAG of Leipzig-Wahren (amongst other firms) with a development contract for a new eight-wheeled chassis with all-wheel drive and steering. It was to have been the Schwerer Einheits Geländegängiger Wehrmachts Lastkraftwagen (heavy standard cross-country Wehrmacht lorry), but it was never adopted for service in this form. At the same time, a requirement for a heavy eight-wheeled armoured car was also issued—and the Büssing-NAG 8 x 8 GS chassis, with a new armoured body, took over the functions of the commercially-built six-wheeled Sd.Kfz.231 series. For this reason, all armoured cars on the GS chassis received the same designation as their six-wheeled predecessors but with the suffix '8-Rad' (8-wheeled) as a distinguishing mark. The car was the most advanced cross-country vehicle that could be built at that time, utilising the latest technological knowledge; and its excellent cross-country ability and high road-speed were achieved only by virtue of a relatively complicated chassis layout.

The Heereswaffenamt made funds available for the development of this eight-wheeled armoured car during 1935, when it was classified as Vs.Kfz (Versuchskraftfahrzeuge or experimental vehicle) 623. Overall control of the development and production of the armoured bodies was undertaken by Deutschen-Werke A.G. in Kiel, and assembly was carried out by F. Schichau in Elbing. The first production batch was delivered to the Wehrmacht during 1937; and this original model was produced until 1938, when it was superseded by an improved model with a new hull design and other minor automotive changes. The major visual difference was the elimination of the facets at the front of the hull and a new turret (on the Sd.Kfz.231 and Sd.Kfz.232) with

a higher frontal plate. Full replacement of the six-wheeled model had not been completed by the beginning of the war, hence its use in early operations. Production of all cars based on the GS chassis ceased during 1942, when the new Sd.Kfz.234 series was introduced. One of its major disadvantages had been its great height, which made it an easy target. The L8V engine continued in production, however, until 1944.

With varying superstructures, the car represented the standard heavy equipment of the armoured reconnaissance companies of the Panzer divisions. A total of 1235 of the following models were produced: Schwerer Panzerspähwagen Sd.Kfz.231 (8-Rad); Schwerer Panzerspähwagen (Fu) Sd.Kfz.232 (8-Rad); Schwerer Panzerspähwagen (7.5cm) Sd.Kfz.233 (8-Rad); Schwerer Panzerfunkwagen Sd.Kfz.263 (8-Rad).

Often referred to as the "Achtrad" (eight-wheeler), the car had all-wheel drive and steering and fully-independent suspension, which gave it a remarkable cross-country performance. Even in the heavy mud of Russia it put up a good show, but its main contribution was in the desert campaign.

Although production was discontinued in 1942, most of these vehicles remained in service until the end of the war and took part in practically all campaigns on all fronts.

The Basic Eight-wheeled GS Vehicle

The armoured hull of this vehicle was of welded construction and was built up on a chassis frame. Of light construction owing to the rigidity of the armoured hull, the chassis frame was mainly the assembly foundation for all the mechanical components and was composed of two parallel Z-section side-members joined by two main tubular cross-members—which also served as the pivots on which the four suspension springs rocked. Auxiliary light cross-members of channel section and the four final drive gearboxes, very rigidly attached to the direct side-members, gave additional strength. The bare chassis weighed 4120kg (4.12 tons).

The early chassis, produced from 1937 to 1938, was

powered by a Büssing-NAG L8V water-cooled V8 petrol engine developing 155bhp at 3000rpm; but later models had it uprated to 180bhp by increasing the bore. The engine was mounted at the front of the frame (often referred to as the rear of the vehicle although, strictly speaking, there was no such thing), and the drive was taken by way of the clutch and a short, jointed coupling-shaft to a centrally-mounted three-speed gearbox that incorporated an auxiliary high/low ratio operated by a separate lever. Two levers made six speed available, however, and these could be used for forward or reverse travel through a direction-change box operated by a foot-pedal. From the gearbox, the drive was taken fore and aft to two reduction boxes—one each for the front and rear bogies—each of which was located between the two axles of a bogie and transmitted the drive to them through a ZF cam-type differential or compensating gear of the free-wheel type. All four axles were driven and steered in this way. Because of the differences in the radii of the circles described by the front, rear and intermediate wheels on full lock, a De Lavaud inter-axle differential was housed in each of the two reduction boxes.

Each of the eight road-wheels was linked to the frame by two swinging links, one above the other; and the upper links were connected in two bogie-pairs per side and sprung on single inverted, semi-elliptic springs pivoted to the frame.

The four-axle steering system was additionally complicated by the provision of front and rear steering wheels and controls. Wheels were of conventional pressed-steel disc three-piece type, carrying low-pressure cord-reinforced cross-country tyres with a self-sealing internal coating to the inner tubes.

Characteristics common to all vehicles on the GS chassis
Weight of chassis: 4120kg (4.12 tons).
Length of chassis: 5780mm (19.0ft).
Width of chassis: 1780mm (5.84ft).
Ground clearance: 270mm (10.6in).
Track (all wheels): 1600mm (5.25ft).
Wheelbase: 1350+1400+1350mm (4.43+4.60+4.43ft).
Wheel width: 190mm (7.5in).
Engine
Make: Büssing-NAG.
Model: L8V-GS petrol.
No. of cylinders: 8 (90°V).
Output: 150hp at 3000rpm.*
Swept volume: 7913cc.*
Cooling: Water (pump).
Carburettor: 2 x Solex 48 FNVP.*
Transmission
Gearbox: Constant mesh, helical gear; three gears plus transfer giving six forward and six reverse ratios.
Drive: All eight wheels. De Lavaud roller free-wheel type inter-axle differentials; ZF cam-type inter-wheel differentials.
Clutch: Twin disc dry-plate.
Steering: Eight-wheel worm and nut; steering wheel inclined at 90°; additional steering controls at rear.
Brakes: Footbrake, mechanical, acting on all eight

wheels; handbrake acting on all eight wheels.
Chassis: Box-shaped frame.
Suspension: Semi-independent with semi-elliptic springs coupling front and rear pairs of wheels on each side. Three-piece pressed-steel disc wheels, mounting cord-reinforced low-pressure bullet-proof cross-country tyres. Tyre size 210 x 18.
Performance
Fuel capacity: 138 litres (30 gallons).
Turning circle diameter: 10.5m (34ft).
Grade ability: 30°.
Wading depth: 1000mm (3.28ft).
Vertical step: 500mm (1.64ft).
Trench crossing ability: 1250mm (4.1ft).
*Cars produced between 1939-42 had the engine bore increased from 107mm to 110mm, making the swept volume 8360cc and giving an output of 180hp at 3000rpm. These vehicles also had two Solex 40 MOVS carburettors.

Armoured car models based on the Eight-wheeled GS Chassis

a. Schwerer Panzerspähwagen (s.Pz.Sp.Wg.) Sd.Kfz.231 (8-Rad) mit GS Fahrgestell für Schwerer Panzerspähwagen: heavy armoured reconnaissance vehicle Sd.Kfz.231 (8-wheeled) with the GS chassis for the heavy armoured reconnaissance vehicle

The heavy eight-wheeled armoured car Sd.Kfz.231 was a weapons vehicle (Waffenwagen), having a fully-rotating turret mounting a 20mm KwK 30 or 38 heavy machine-gun and a coaxial 7.92mm MG-34. A 9mm MP-38 or 40 machine-pistol was also carried for protection at close quarters. The vehicle was equipped with wireless, the aerial being of the rod type; and the crew consisted of four men—a commander, a gunner and two drivers.

The main hull was divided into two sections bolted together at a vertical flanged joint approximately in line with the radiator, the rear section readily detachable for access to the engine. Both sections were of welded construction, employing face-hardened armour plate. The whole of the hull interior was well arranged for stowage and there was ample space for the crew. The front driver had a fairly wide field of vision, but the length of the engine-cover curtailed the rear driver's line of sight.

The turret was constructed of single-skin face-hardened armour plate, and all plates were joined by welding. The seats for the commander and gunner were mounted on a tubular framework suspended from the turret, thus eliminating the need for a rotating floor. The left-hand seat was intended for the commander, who had a periscope that could be swung into position when required; and there were periscope attachments for a camera that could be used on reconnaissance missions. The turret rotated on a large diameter ball-bearing seated on an internal spur gear ring that was bolted to the top of the hull. Two independent means were provided for rotating the turret. There was a high-geared quick-acting auxiliary control at the left of the commander, and the gunner controlled a separate combined gear for rotating the turret with greater accuracy and for elevating the guns.

Some early cars had an extra shield 10mm thick fitted about two feet in front of the hull to increase protection. The space between the shield and the front of the hull, at the sides and bottom, was enclosed by perforated plates so that it could be used for stowage. The later version, having the up-rated engine, dispensed with this and the thickness of the nose-plate and gun-mantlet was increased to 30mm.

Characteristics (in addition to those of the basic GS chassis)
Weight, unladen: 7550kg (7.55 tons).
Weight, fully laden: 8300kg (8.3 tons).
Axle loadings, front two axles: 2050kg (2.05 tons) each.
Axle loadings, rear two axles: 2100kg 2.1 tons) each.
Crew: Four men (commander, gunner, two drivers).
Length, overall: 5850mm (19.18ft) (without front pannier).
Width, overall: 2200mm (7.22ft).
Height, overall: 2340mm (7.66ft).
Armour
Type: Flat, face-hardened armour steel, welded, proof against light anti-tank guns.
Hull: Nose, 8+10mm (2ft space), later 30mm; glacis, 5mm; sides, 8-10mm; rear, 10mm; roof, 5mm; floor, 5mm.
Turret: Front, 8mm-15mm (later 30mm); sides, 8mm; rear, 8mm; roof, 5mm.
Armament
One 2cm Kwk 30 or 38 ⎰ Both mounted coaxially in flat
One 7.92mm MG-34 ⎱ mantlet and both fired by pedals on gunner's foot-rest.
One 9mm MP-38 or MP-40 machine-pistol.
One 27mm signal pistol.
Six stick hand-grenades.
Turret
Traverse: 360°, mechanically assisted.
Elevation: −10° to +26°.
Ammunition
2cm: 180 rounds.
7.92mm: 2100 rounds.
9mm: 192 rounds.
27mm signal cartridges: 12.
Performance
Maximum speed, road: 85kph (53mph).
Maximum speed, cross-country: 30kph (19mph).
Radius of action, road: 270km (170 miles).
Radius of action, cross-country: 150km (95 miles).
Communication: R/T, rod-type aerial.
Sighting and Vision: Coaxial sighting telescope T.Z.F.6., commander's periscope; vision openings with laminated glass and armour flaps.

b. Schwerer Panzerspähwagen (s.Pz.Sp.Wg.) Sd.Kfz.232 (Fu) (8-Rad) mit GS Fahrgestell für Schwerer Panzerspähwagen: heavy armoured reconnaissance vehicle Sd.Kfz.232 (wireless) with the GS chassis for the heavy armoured reconnaissance vehicle
This was the Funkwagen version of the eight-wheeled armoured car—identical to the Sd.Kfz.231 (8-Rad) as regards its armament and traversing turret. The

medium-range wireless equipment, however, was provided with a large frame-aerial mounted horizontally above the turret, extending approximately the whole length of the vehicle and curved down at each end. It was mounted on a pivot above the turret at the front and on two stays at the rear of the vehicle. The pivot mounting at the front allowed the turret to traverse; but when traversed to the rear, there was a danger of shooting away the supporting stays at low elevation and the rear of the aerial at high elevation. Like the Sd.Kfz.231 (8-Rad), this vehicle had a crew of four.

In later models, the horizontal frame-aerial was replaced by a rod-aerial on the turret roof and a star-aerial on the centre of the rear deck. The radio equipment in this vehicle was expensive and very complicated, and it therefore proved difficult to maintain.

Characteristics (differing from those of the Sd.Kfz.231 (8-Rad)
Weight, unladen: 7700kg (7.70 tons).
Weight, fully laden: 8800kg (8.80 tons).
Axle loadings (all axles): 2275kg (2.3 tons).
Height, overall: 2900mm (9.50ft).
Armament: As for Sd.Kfz.231 but with the omission of the 7.62mm coaxial machine-gun.
Communication: R/T and W/T (medium-range) transmitter and receiver.

c. Schwerer Panzerspähwagen (s.Pz.Sp.Wg.) (7.5cm) Sd.Kfz.233 mit GS Fahrgestell für Schwerer Panzerspähwagen: heavy armoured reconnaissance vehicle (7.5cm gun) Sd.Kfz.233 with the GS chassis for the heavy armoured reconnaissance vehicle
This vehicle was introduced to increase the offensive power of armoured reconnaissance units. It entered service during October 1942, following an order for the mounting of the Stummelkanone of the Sturmgeschütz III and the Pz.Kpfw.IV tank on the eight-wheeled armoured car chassis. The vehicle consisted of a short 7.5cm Kwk 37 L/24 gun mounted in a turretless eight-wheeled armoured car chassis. The weapon had only limited traverse. It was provided with a dial sight on the left, and it fired high-explosive, smoke and two types of armour-piercing round. The vehicle had a three-man crew — commander-gunner/wireless-operator; loader/rear driver; and front driver.

Characteristics (in addition to those of the basic GS chassis)
Weight, unladen: 7550kg (7.55 tons).
Weight, fully laden: 8580kg (8.58 tons).
Axle loadings (all axles): 2145kg (2.15 tons).
Crew: Three men (commander, rear driver, front driver).
Length, overall: 5850mm (19.18ft).
Width, overall: 2200mm (7.22ft).
Height, overall: 2250mm (7.38ft)—some models 2500mm (8.2ft).
Armour
Hull: As for Sd.Kfz.231 (8-Rad).
Superstructure: 10mm all round.
Armament

7.5cm Kwk 37 L/24 gun.
7.92mm MP-38 or MP-40.
27mm signal pistol (later replaced by smoke dischargers).

Ammunition
7.5cm: 55 rounds of HE, smoke and AP.
7.92mm: 2100 rounds.
Smoke canisters: 12.

Performance
Maximum speed, road: 85kph (53mph).
Maximum speed, cross-country: 30kph (19mph).
Radius of action, road: 300km (190 miles).
Radius of action, cross-country: 150km (95 miles).
Communication: R/T, rod-type aerial.
Sighting and Vision: Dial sight; commander's periscope; vision openings with laminated glass and armour flaps.

---

d. Schwerer Panzerfunkwagen (s.Pz.Fu.Wg.) Sd.Kfz.263 (8-Rad) mit GS Fahrgestell für Schwerer Panzerspähwagen: heavy armoured wireless vehicle Sd.Kfz.263 with the GS Chassis for the heavy armoured reconnaissance vehicle

This long-range command vehicle had no rotating turret, thus allowing a roomy body for the crew and the medium-wave radio equipment (originally 100w, later 80w). It was used by the signals platoons of armoured reconnaissance units and signals battalions.

The fixed turret was slightly larger than the turrets of the other models, and the angles of its sides conformed to the upper hull sides and were integral with them. The turret was closed by an armoured roof. Hulls for these vehicles were produced only by Deutschen-Werke in Kiel. The car originally carried a large overhead frame aerial of the same general type as that fitted to the Sd.Kfz.232 (8-Rad), but on later vehicles it was replaced by a rod-type aerial. The frame aerial was supported by two stays at the centre. One MG-34 gun could be fitted. When fitted, the machine-gun was mounted in a ball mounting at the front of the superstructure.

Of the vehicle's two drivers, the rear one doubled as radio operator.

The vehicle entered production during 1937, but during January 1942 production was halted in favour of the semi-tracked models.

Characteristics (in addition to those of the basic GS chassis)
Weight, unladen: 7550kg (7.55 tons).
Weight, fully laden: 8680kg (8.68 tons).
Axle loadings (all axles): 2170kg (2.17 tons).
Crew: Five men (two of them drivers).
Length, overall: 5850mm (19.18ft).
Width, overall: 2200mm (7.22ft).
Height, overall: 2900mm (9.5ft).
Armour
Hull: As for Sd.Kfz.231 (8-Rad).
Superstructure: 10mm all round.
Armament
Optional 7.92mm MG-34 in ball-mounting at front of superstructure.
One MP-38 or MP-40 machine-carbine.

Ammunition
7.92mm: 1000 rounds.
9mm: 192 rounds.
Performance
Maximum speed, road: 85kph (53mph).
Maximum speed, cross-country: 30kph (19mph).
Radius of action, road: 300km (190 miles).
Radius of action, cross-country: 150km (95 miles).
Communication: Long-range W/T transmitter and receiver.
Sighting and Vision: Open sight on gun; normal vision slits.

---

2. Schwerer Panzerspähwagen (heavy armoured reconnaissance car) 8 x 8 (Sd.Kfz.234 series)

On 5th August 1940 the Heereswaffenamt placed an order with Büssing-NAG for an eight-wheeled reconnaissance vehicle as a successor to the original GS type. The new vehicle was to be similar to the original but having a monocoque hull in place of the chassis and to be better suited to operation in hot climates. To satisfy the latter condition, the Tatra firm in Nesseldorf received an order for the development of a 12-cylinder V, 14.8L diesel engine developing 220hp at 2250rpm. Hitherto, all German armoured cars had been powered by petrol engines. Despite the early start, this 'tropical' vehicle did not enter production until 1944.

Parent firm for the chassis and hull was Büssing-NAG of Berlin-Oberschöneweide but the chassis itself was built by Büssing-NAG of Leipzig and received the manufacturer's designation ARK. The armoured hull was produced by Deutschen Edelstahlwerke in Krefeld, and the turret (where fitted) was by Daimler-Benz AG and F. Schichau in Elbing.

The first trial vehicle, which weighed 10 tons, was delivered to the Wehrmacht in July 1941; but the original engine gave great trouble and so an improved model (Tatra 103) was built with special provisions to restrict noise. The third, and final, tropical engine was to have been delivered during 1942; but with the termination of the African campaign it was not pursued. Entering production during 1943, the vehicle appeared in the following variants: Schwerer Panzerspähwagen (2cm) Sd.Kfz.234/1; Schwerer Panzerspähwagen (5cm) Sd.Kfz.234/2; Schwerer Panzerspähwagen (7.5cm kurz) Sd.Kfz.234/3; Schwerer Panzerspähwagen (7.5cm lang) Sd.Kfz.234/4.

The vehicles had thicker armour than the earlier GS series. Frontal thickness on the hull and turret (where fitted) was 30mm, on the hull sides 8mm, on the turret sides and rear 14.5mm, and on the hull rear 10mm. The hull roof and turret roof were 10mm thick. With the diesel engine and the larger (270-20) tyres, the range with a full fuel tank was 600km—which greatly increased the tactical value of the vehicle. Later production models had the fuel tank capacity increased to 360 litres, giving a range of operation of up to 1000km.

During 1944, the armoured reconnaissance vehicles of the ARK series replaced the GS series. Although originally intended for use by the Afrika Korps, they entered service too late but were used with great effect in Russia and north-west Europe. A total of about 2300 were built, and they were the last armoured cars to be produced for the Wehrmacht. The Sd.Kfz.234 series constituted the only wheeled armoured car scheduled for the March 1945 production programme. It was to have been produced at the rate of 100 vehicles per month and was the only reconnaissance vehicle to be continued apart from the special model of the Pz.Kpfw.38(t).

The Sd.Kfz.234 vehicle was externally similar to the earlier Sd.Kfz.234 vehicle except that the monocoque hull made it much lower, and the orginal four mudguards were replaced by two long fenders—one on each side—each containing four panniers. The overall weight of the various models was between 10.5 and 11.5 tons. The general automotive layout remained unaltered but for the fact that Knorr pneumatic foot-brakes were used in place of the original mechanical type of the GS vehicle.

Characteristics common to all vehicles on the ARK chassis
Weight of chassis: 8000kg (8.0 tons).
Length of chassis: 6000mm (19.68ft, arbitrary measurement).
Width of chassis: 2145mm (7.04ft, arbitrary measurement).
Ground clearance: 350mm (13.8in).
Track (all wheels): 1945mm (6.39ft).
Wheelbase: 1300+1400+1300mm (4.26+4.60+4.26ft).
Wheel width: 190mm (7.5in).
Engine
Make: Tatra.
Model: 103 diesel.
No. of cylinders: 12 (75°V).
Output: 210hp at 2250rpm.
Swept volume: 14825cc.
Cooling: Air (compressor).
Carburettor: Two Bosch PE 6A fuel injection pumps.
Transmission
Gearbox: Constant mesh, helical gear; three gears plus transfer, giving six forward and six reverse ratios.
Drive: All eight wheels. De Lavaud roller free-wheel-type inter-axle differentials; ZF cam-type inter-wheel differentials.
Clutch: Twin disc dry-plate.
Steering: Eight-wheel worm and nut; steering wheel inclined at 90°; additional steering controls at rear.
Brakes: Foot-brake, Knorr pneumatic, acting on all eight wheels. Hand-brake acting on all eight wheels.
Chassis: Monocoque.
Suspension: Semi-independent with semi-elliptic springs coupling front and rear pairs of wheels on each side. Three-piece pressed-steel disc wheels, mounting cord-reinforced low-pressure bullet-proof cross-country tyres. Tyre size 270 x 20.
Performance
Fuel capacity: 240 litres (later 360 litres) (53 gallons, later 80 gallons).
Turning circle diameter: 14.9m (49ft).
Grade ability: 30°.

Wading depth: 1200mm (3.9ft).
Vertical step: 500mm (1.64ft).
Trench crossing ability: 1350mm (4.42ft).

Armoured car models based on the Eight-wheeled ARK Chassis

a. Schwerer Panzerspähwagen (s.Pz.Sp.Wg.) (2cm) Sd.Kfz.234/1 mit ARK Fahrgestell für Schwerer Panzerspähwagen: heavy armoured reconnaissance vehicle (2cm gun) Sd.Kfz.234/1 with the ARK chassis for the heavy armoured reconnaissance vehicle

This was a commander's eight-wheeled armoured car mounting a 2cm gun. It was fitted with an open-topped fully-rotating six-sided turret, similar to that used on the armoured semi-tracked vehicle Sd.Kfz.250/9. This turret reduced the overall height, and the mounting was designed to cater for anti-aircraft protection. Frontal plates of the turret were 30mm thick, and the sides were 8mm thick. The main armament was a centrally-mounted 2cm Kwk 38 with an MG-42 coaxially mounted on the left. Both guns were fired from levers hinged to the forward side of the elevation and traverse hand-wheel by means of Bowden cables. The right-hand lever controlled the 2cm Kwk 38, the left-hand one the MG-42. Stowage space was provided for twenty-four 20-round magazines along the left-hand side of the hull, and a folding wire-mesh anti-grenade screen was fitted to the turret top. The vehicle was produced from 1944-5.

Characteristics (in addition to those of the basic ARK chassis)
Weight, unladen: 9800kg (9.8 tons).
Weight, fully laden: 10500kg (10.5 tons).
Axle loadings (all axles): 2625kg (2.63 tons).
Crew: Four men (commander, gunner, two drivers).
Length, overall: 6020mm (19.7ft).
Width, overall: 2360mm (7.75ft).
Height, overall: 2100mm (6.88ft).
Armour
Type: Flat face-hardened armour steel, welded, proof against light anti-tank guns.
Hull: Nose, 30mm; glacis, 17mm; sides, 10mm; rear, 9mm; roof, 9mm; floor, 9mm.
Turret: Front, 30mm; sides, 8mm; rear, 8mm; roof, open.
Armament
One 2cm Kwk 38
One 7.92mm MG-42
coaxially mounted.
Turret
Traverse: 360° mechanically assisted.
Elevation: 0°-75°.
Ammunition
2cm: 480 rounds.
7.92mm: 2400 rounds.
Performance
Maximum speed, road: 85kph (53mph).
Maximum speed, cross-country: 30kph (19mph).
Radius of action, road: Originally 600km (375 miles), later 1000km (625 miles).
Radius of action, cross-country: Originally 330km (200

miles), later 550km (350 miles).
Communication: W/T, R/T, intercom.
Sighting and Vision: T.Z.F.3a. telescopic sight and Flie-gervisier (aircraft visor) 38 for anti-aircraft defence. Numerous vision slits around hull and turret with bullet-proof laminated glass blocks.

---

b. Schwerer Panzerspähwagen (s.Pz.Sp.Wg.) (5cm) Sd.Kfz.234/2 Puma mit ARK Fahrgestell für Schwerer Panzerspähwagen: heavy armoured reconnaissance vehicle (5cm gun) Sd.Kfz.234/2 Puma with the ARK chassis for the heavy armoured reconnaissance vehicle

Because of the light and medium tanks in Soviet recon-naissance units, the Heereswaffenamt requested the development of a new armoured car model mounting a gun capable of penetrating such armour in a defen-sive situation (that is at close range). As a result, the Sd.Kfz.234 chassis was reworked and fitted with the turret originally intended for the Leopard light tank, mounting the 5cm Kwk 39/1 L/60 anti-tank gun and coaxial MG-42. The new armoured car was designated Sd.Kfz.234/2 Puma.

The turret was oval-shaped with steeply-sloping sides, providing an excellent ballistic shape. The gun, fitted with a muzzle-brake, had a muzzle-velocity of 2,700fps when firing armour-piercing ammunition. It had a verti-cal sliding breech-block and was semi-automatic. A spring-type equilibriator was mounted on the right-hand side, between the cradle and the turret roof. The hydro-pneumatic recoil mechanism was mounted in the mant-let on top of the piece. The mantlet was cast in one piece, somewhat similar in appearance to that on the later German assault guns, but the casting also included the coaxial machine-gun. The T.Z.F.4b telescopic sight was used; and six smoke-projectors were mounted—three on each side of the turret.

Characteristics (in addition to those for the basic ARK chassis)
Weight, unladen: 11500kg (11.5 tons).
Weight, fully laden: 11740kg (11.74 tons).
Axle loadings (all axles): 2935 kg (2.94 tons).
Crew: Four men (commander, gunner, two drivers).
Length, overall (including gun): 6800mm (22.3ft).
Length, excluding gun: 6000m (19.7ft).
Width, overall: 2330mm (7.55ft).
Height, overall: 2380mm (7.8ft).
Armour
Type: As for Sd.Kfz.234/1.
Hull: As for Sd.Kfz.234/1.
Turret: Front, 30mm (mantlet 40-100mm); sides, 10mm; rear, 10mm; roof, 10mm.
Armament
One 5cm Kwk 39/1 L/60 anti-tank gun
One MG-42 7.92mm machine-gun
coaxially mounted.
Six smoke projectors, three on each side of turret.
Turret
Traverse: 360°, manual.
Elevation: −7° to +25°.
Ammunition

5cm: 55 rounds (27 APCBC, 28 HE).
7.92mm: 1980 rounds.
Performance
Maximum speed, road: 85kph (53mph).
Maximum speed, cross-country: 30kph (19mph).
Radius of action, road: Originally 600km (375 miles), later 1000km (625 miles).
Radius of action, cross-country: Originally 330km (200 miles), later 550km (350 miles).
Communication: Fu.Spr.f. R/T; could also have long-range equipment Fu.12. Two aerials—one on the turret roof and the other on the left-hand vehicle side.
Sighting and Vision: Sight T.Z.F.46. Two-way periscope with 360° traverse, mounted in turret hatches, for gun-ner and commander. Another periscope for commander in turret roof, forward of his hatch. Normal vision ports with laminated glass blocks.

---

c. Schwerer Panzerspähwagen (s.Pz.Sp.Wg.) (7.5cm kurz) Sd.Kfz.234/3 mit ARK Fahrgestell für Schwerer Panzerspähwagen: heavy armoured reconnaissance vehicle (7.5cm short gun) Sd.Kfz.234/3 with the ARK chassis for the heavy armoured reconnaissance vehicle

Even with the 5cm gun on the Puma armoured car, German reconnaissance units were hard pressed to effectively combat Soviet armour. Therefore, at Hitler's personal request, a limited traverse mounted 75mm short tank gun was installed. The armament consisted of a 7.5cm K51 or K51/1 (L/24), facing forward over the front of the vehicle, mounted with limited traverse above the driver in a fixed turret. This new model, desig-nated Sd.Kfz.234/3, took over the role of the earlier Sd.Kfz.233 model based on the GS chassis.

Characteristics (in addition to those of the basic ARK Chassis)
Weight, unladen: 9700kg (9.7 tons).
Weight, fully laden: 10000kg (10.00 tons) .
Axle loadings (all axles): 2500kg (2.50 tons).
Crew: Four men (two gunners, two drivers).
Length, overall (including gun): 6000mm (19.7ft).
Length, excluding gun: 6000mm (19.7ft).
Width, overall: 2330mm (7.55ft).
Height, overall: 2362mm (7.75ft).
Armour
Type: As for Sd.Kfz.234/1.
Hull: As for Sd.Kfz.234/1.
Superstructure: Front, 30mm; sides, 10mm.
Armament
7.5cm K51 or K51/1 (L/24) short tank-gun.
7.62mm MG-42 sometimes fitted.
Turret None.
Ammunition
7.5cm: 55 rounds.
7.92mm: 1980 rounds (when fitted).
Performance
Maximum speed, road 85kph (53mph).
Maximum speed, cross-country: 30kph (19 mph).
Radius of action, road: Originally 600km (375 miles), later 1000km (625 miles).
Radius of action, cross-country: Originally 330km (200

miles), later 550km (350 miles).
Communication: W/T and R/T.
Sighting and Vision: Conventional artillery dial sight on gun; normal vision slits around hull.

---

d. Schwerer Panzerspähwagen (s.Pz.Sp.Wg.) (7.5cm lang) Sd.Kfz.234/4 mit ARK Fahrgestell für Schwerer Panzerspähwagen: heavy armoured reconnaissance vehicle (7.5cm long gun) Sd.Kfz.234/4 with the ARK chassis for the heavy armoured reconnaissance vehicle
This vehicle was also personally ordered by Hitler and

was practically identical to the Sd.Kfz.234/3 except for the longer gun. Only a few trial vehicles were produced, but they did take part in operations.

The complete carriage with barrel and shield of the 7.5cm Pak 40 (L/48) was mounted, unaltered, on a pivot at the centre of the fighting compartment. The vehicle was often referred to as the Pak-Wagen (anti-tank vehicle).

Apart from a few minor dimensions (related to the change in armament), the characteristics of this vehicle were the same as those of the Sd.Kfz.234/3.

▲143

144▼

143, 144. Büssing-NAG GS chassis for the 8-wheeled armoured car. **Sd.Kfz.231 (8 Rad)**

145. Note the spaced armoured stowage bin on the front of the vehicle.

146. In Russia. The front stowage bin is being used to hold wood palings.

147. Armoured cars, and the Funk version, on a reconnaissance mission in Russia.

▲145

▲146

147 ▼

▲148

▲149

150▼

Sd.Kfz.231 (8 Rad)

148. Armoured cars guarding Russian prisoners.

149. An early vehicle with a swastika painted on the front stowage bin.

150. A view that clearly shows the shape of the spaced frontal armour and the various vision and hatch arrangements.

151. Note the perforation in the side of the stowage bin, to reduce the weight. The four rods — one at each corner — are to enable the driver to judge the width of the car when driving.

152. A vehicle knocked out of action in Europe following the D-Day operations.

▲ 153

▲ 154   155 ▼

153. A view showing the detail on top of the 8-wheeled armoured car.
154. The space between the wheels, in the mudguards, was used for the stowing of tools — the flaps to the compartments being evident here.
155. The vehicle of an SS unit negotiating steep terrain.
156. Camouflage-painted, in action. Note external stowage of steel helmets.
157. Preparing to go into action.

▲156

157 ▼

158, 159. Taking part in operations.
160. The entrance doors, between the two mudguards, can be clearly seen here.
161. A captured vehicle with its turret traversed to the rear.

▲158   159▼

162. An Sd.Kfz.231 (8 Rad) with the Afrika Korps. It has a rod-type aerial attached to the turret.

163. An Sd.Kfz.232 (Fu) (8 Rad) armoured radio car with spaced armour on the front.

164. A version of the Sd.Kfz.232 (8 Rad) with no spaced armour on the front.

165. A captured Sd.Kfz.232 (8 Rad) of the Afrika Korps being inspected by 8th Army soldiers.

▲162

163▼

▲164

165▼

Sd.Kzf.232 (8 Rad)

166. A plate has been welded over the rear radiator grille of this vehicle.

167. As is evidenced here, tools were sometimes attached to the spaced armour frontal plate.

168. Operating in conjunction with an engineers unit.

169. On a reconnaissance mission in Russia, obviously moving at speed.

▲168

169▼

▲170
171▼

Sd.Kfz.232 (8 Rad)
170. An interesting view of the wheel alignment as the vehicle turns to the left.
171. Large numbers of these vehicles were allotted to Panzer divisions, as this divisional vehicle park indicates.
172. This view of an SS unit vehicle shows how easily the traverse of the gun could be fouled by the aerial stays.
173. A vehicle 'opened up'.

Sd.Kfz.232 (8 Rad)

174. Close-up of turret details, with the hull entrance doors also in evidence.

175. Operating in conjunction with an Sd.Kfz.233 'Stummelkanone'.

176. The vehicle seen in fine detail.

177. In transit to the Russian front.

▲ 175

▲ 176

177 ▼

◄ 174

178. An early vehicle taking part in a parade in Germany.
179. An SS division vehicle.
180. Later model of Sd.Kfz.232 (Fu) (8 Rad) with star aerial attached to the rear of the hull.
181. In action. The mounting for the star aerial can be clearly seen.
182. Another view of the vehicle at rest.

▲178

▲179

180▼

WH - 237 778

Sd.Kfz.233

183. Front view of the Sd.Kfz.233, mounting a 7.5cm KwK.

184. A captured vehicle. Note the sighting periscope to the rear of the 7.5cm mounting.

185. A heavily camouflaged vehicle in action with the Afrika Korps.

186. In the desert, with the Afrika Korps. (The licence number was probably painted out in the photograph for security reasons.)

187. Another captured vehicle.

▲185

▲186

187 ▼

▲188

Sd.Kfz.233
188. A German official photograph.
189. An Afrika Korps vehicle fitted with an MG-34 for anti-aircraft defence.
190. In action in Europe.
191. A close-up showing the armament and sighting arrangements.
192. A later model. Note the raised superstructure around the fighting compartment.

▲189   190▼

WH-1451426

WH-143179

Sd.Kfz.263

193. The s.Pz.SP.Fu.Wg. Sd.Kfz.263 8-wheeled radio car.

194. A front view showing the MG-34 mounting and the fixed turret built out of the armoured hull.

195. Taking part in a parade.

196. In action with a reconnaissance unit in the Low Countries.

197. With the Afrika Korps. The MG-34 is protected by a canvas sleeve.

 ▲195

 ▲196   197 ▼

▲ 198

Sd.Kfz.263

198. A side view showing how the turret is formed out of the upper hull armour. The MG has been removed from this vehicle.

199. In action with the Afrika Korps.

200. Driving in column with the Afrika Korps.

201. A three-quarters rear view.

202. In action in Russia.

203. A rare photograph showing the armoured top of the vehicle.

▲ 199   200 ▼

▲ 201

▲ 202

203 ▼

115

WH-215795

▲206

207▼

Sd.Kfz.263
204. With turret hatches open.
205. In action, crossing a repaired bridge.
206. Negotiating a river, camouflaged with branches.
207. Travelling at speed in action.

▲ 210

211 ▼

Sd.Kfz.263

208. Taking part in a march-past before Hitler.

209. In action in Russia.

210, 211. During the Warsaw uprising of 1944. The star aerial is in use on both vehicles.

Sd.Kfz.234/1

212. Commander's armoured car with the turret traversed to the rear. Note the new-style mudguards and the lower profile in comparison with the Sd.Kfz.231 (8 Rad) series.

213. Plan view showing the interior of the turret and the rear engine deck arrangement.

214. Rare photograph of the Sd.Kfz.234/1 in action in Russia. The grenade screens — very much like those on the Sd.Kfz.222 — have been opened out.

215. Here the second wheel from the rear has been bolted up because of broken suspension units. It is not the normal wheel position.

▲ 214

215 ▼

Sd.Kfz.234/2
216. The armoured car known as the 'Puma'.
217. With the body, turret and armament camouflage-painted.
218. A 'Puma' in action in Europe.
219. The 'Puma' was a much lower and more streamlined vehicle than the Sd.Kfz.232, as is evident here.
220. Three-quarters front view showing the conical gun mantlet.

▲ 216

▲ 217   218 ▼

▲ 221

222 ▼

221. Sd.Kfz.234/2 'Puma' armoured car.

222. The Sd.Kfz.234/3, mounting a short 7.5cm gun. This vehicle was designed as a replacement for the Sd.Kfz.233.

223, 224. Further views of the Sd.Kfz.234/3, the second one clearly showing the gun mounting.

▲223

224▼

▲ 225

226 ▼

225, 226. Front and rear views of the Sd.Kfz.234/3, the latter showing the radiator grille and new rear plate.
227, 228. The s.Pz.SP.Wg. Sd.Kfz.234/4 heavy armoured car with long 7.5cm gun.

229, 230. An armoured artillery observation vehicle, based on the Sd.Kfz.234 chassis, used at Hillesleben proving ground.

▲229   230▼